h Century

ne

n

omy

ion

ank

anghai Bank

n

25. Jardine, Matheson & Co., Ltd.
26. Chinese Customs
27. Residence of Xu Tong
28. Hatamen
29. Qianmen
30. Imbeck's Hotel and Store
31. Sanguan Miao
32. Kierulff's Store
33. Spanish Legation
34. Chamot's Peking Hotel

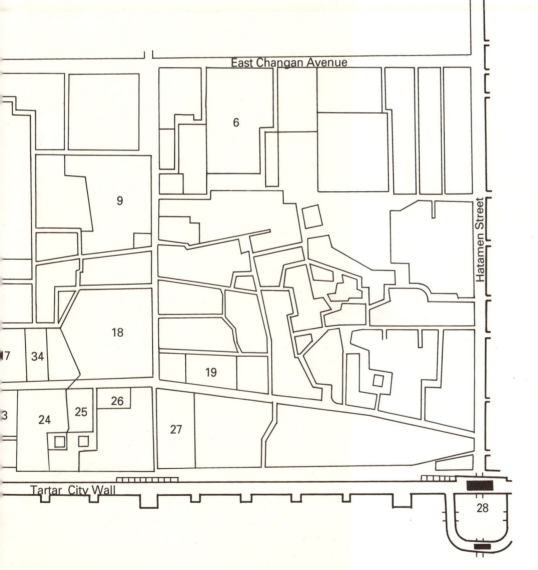

FOREIGNERS WITHIN THE GATES
The Legations at Peking

FOREIGNERS WITHIN THE GATES
The Legations at Peking

MICHAEL J. MOSER
YEONE WEI-CHIH MOSER

HONG KONG
OXFORD UNIVERSITY PRESS
OXFORD   NEW YORK
1993

Oxford University Press, Hong Kong

Oxford   New York   Toronto
Delhi   Bombay   Calcutta   Madras   Karachi
Kuala Lumpur   Singapore   Hong Kong   Tokyo
Nairobi   Dar es Salaam   Cape Town
Melbourne   Auckland   Madrid

and associated companies in
Berlin   Ibadan

Oxford is a trade mark of Oxford University Press

First published 1993

Published in the United States
by Oxford University Press, New York

© Oxford University Press 1993

British Library Cataloguing in Publication Data
available

Library of Congress Cataloging in Publication Data
Moser, Michael J.
Foreigners within the gates: the legations at Peking/Michael J. Moser.
Yeone Wei-chih Moser.
p. cm.
ISBN 0-19-585702-X: $20.00 (est.)
1. Diplomatic and consular service–China.
2. Peking (China)–History.
I. Moser, Yeone Wei-chih. 1975- II. Title.
JX1838.A58P456 1993
351.89'2'0951156–dc20
92-39882
CIP

Printed in Hong Kong
Published by Oxford University Press
18/F Warwick House, Tong Chong Street, Quarry Bay, Hong Kong

獻給

韋德立

李淑娟

Preface

DURING A NEARLY five-year period of residence in Peking beginning in the early 1980s, we had the good fortune to have lived for a time in a magnificent old brick house not far from Tiananmen Square. Nestling behind inconspicuous grey walls, it sat in a compound which included a number of imposing buildings. These were all constructed in the European style popular at the turn of the century, as was our house. To complete the picture, the house was surrounded by several large trees and lay opposite a well-tended flower garden.

The circumstances were exceptional to be sure, especially by comparison with what was then the normal standard of accommodation for foreigners in the Chinese capital. Foreign businessmen, scholars and students were typically housed in Spartan facilities. In the best case these amounted to a two-room suite in a rapidly aging Chinese hotel. The unlucky found themselves in a rectangular cell-like room in some building on the outskirts of Peking built by and for Soviet construction workers in the 1950s.

By a happy set of circumstances, too long and complicated—as are all things in China—to recount here, in late 1983 we obtained a 'lease' over the ground floor of the house. The unwritten agreement with our landlord provided that we might stay as long as two conditions were met. The first was that we make payment on a daily basis. The second required us to maintain an adequate supply of English cigarettes and American coffee for the various 'managers' of the compound who came to our house on a regular basis to enquire about our well-being. It seemed a fair contract, and for nearly two years we made the red brick house our home. We left, reluctantly, to take up a flat in a new high-rise which had just been built for 'foreign guests'.

To Michael, the father of the house, residence in what was then called No. 14 State Guest-house was a special privilege. It meant having the ability to cook one's own meals (if only in a small make-shift kitchen) and the space to put an old piano. By virtue of its location along a long narrow street lined on both sides by old trees, living in the red brick house also provided the opportunity for a daily jog in a section of Peking where cars and trucks were few.

For Yeone, the older daughter of the family, the big house meant different things—as, of course, it would to someone who was then only eight or nine years old. For one thing, it meant companionship, albeit from an unexpected source. At that time, all foreigners in China were vaguely under suspicion. Accordingly, a young boy, no more than sixteen or seventeen years old, 'came with' the house. Dressed in a white linen coat like a waiter on a train, and wearing black cloth shoes, he was our 'service person' or *fuwu yuan*. We called him 'the *fu*' for short. He never really provided any noticeable service, but he drifted freely in and out of the various rooms, presumably to keep watch over us. By the time we left the house, the *fu* had turned into a fine playmate, good with a ball and willing to learn how to make a snowman off in the garden by the side of the house.

Over time, we came to learn about our house—the first secretary's residence in the former Belgian Legation—and the other buildings in our compound, and also about the colourful and very special history of the neighbourhood in which it sat. On Sundays we often spent our afternoons walking up and down the long street at the back of our house—old 'Legation Street'—in search of buildings and places mentioned in the books written about the city's past. Some years later, father and daughter decided to put together a collection of old photographs and write out the story of Peking's old Legation Quarter. The result is this book.

Needless to say, this book is not intended as a detailed or scholarly study of the Legation Quarter and its history. A busy lawyer and a busier high-school student would hardly have time for such a pursuit. However, we do hope that the pages that follow will be of interest to all those who, like us, have a special affection for Peking and its people. We also hope that the book will, at least in a small way, help to keep alive something of the history of this fast-disappearing section of the Chinese capital.

We have many people to thank for helping us to make this book become a reality. First, and always, our thanks go to our family: Yvonne Yi-Feng Wei, wife and mother; Anna-Sieglinde, daughter and younger sister; and Christa Isolde, daughter number three and youngest sister. Although Anna was just an infant when we lived in the old Legation Quarter and Christa was not yet born, both have, in the years since our departure, visited the places described in this book on numerous occasions as our work progressed.

We would also like to express our thanks to the following individuals and institutions: Dr Lai-bing Kan, Chief Librarian of the University of Hong Kong Libraries, for kindly granting us access to many of the valuable books kept in the library's special collection; research staff at the Oriental and India Office Collections of the British Library and the Bettmann Archive; Soshan Cheung and Susan Smith for their assistance in locating hard-to-find materials; Andrew Andreasen, who provided the early inspiration for the book; the late Mrs Hedda Morrison for sharing with us her recollections of life in the Legation Quarter; the Beijing International Society; and Yaoqun Song, faithful comrade, intrepid driver, omniscient teacher and loyal friend whose patience with our many demands has been richly rewarded by the fact that he now knows the entire Legation Quarter inch by inch. We would also like to thank June Chen and Dorothy Tang for their assistance in typing the manuscript. Needless to say, any errors or omissions found in the book are solely ours.

Finally, we would like to acknowledge our special debt to Jeanne Shu-chuan Lee and Luis Te-li Wei, to whom this book is dedicated. In a very real sense it was they who first set us down the road to Peking.

MICHAEL J. MOSER
YEONE WEI-CHIH MOSER
Hong Kong
and
Nantucket Island
Summer 1992

Contents

Preface   *vii*
Maps   *xii*
Figures   *xii*
Acknowledgements and Credits   *xiii*

1. Foreigners in the Middle Kingdom   1

2. The Early Legations   13

3. Peking and the Foreign Community in
   the Nineteenth Century   27

4. The Siege of the Legations   41

5. The Aftermath   69

6. The Protocol of 1901   85

7. Rebuilding the Legation Quarter   93

8. The Legations and Their World: 1901–1949   111

9. Postscript   141

Glossary of Chinese Terms   152
Bibliography   153
Index   156

Maps

1. The Legation Quarter in the Late
   Nineteenth Century   *Front Endpaper*
2. The City of Peking in the Late Nineteenth Century   12
3. The Legation Quarter in 1915   *Back Endpaper*

Figures

1. Rates of Exchange, 1901   89
2. The Public and Private Claims of the Powers,
   as Estimated on 1 July 1901, and as Finally
   Settled in the Protocol   90

Acknowledgements and Credits

The photographs contained in this book were assembled from a variety of sources, including private collections, photographic libraries, old books, and flea market albums. A special debt is owed to the following for their kind permission to reproduce photographs set out in the book:

Anne Selby Productions 94, 96, 97 [top], 100 [bottom], 102 [bottom], 105, 106 [top], 107, 112; The BBC Hulton Picture Library (Hulton-Deutsch Collection) 39, 69, 77 [top], 80, 93, 114; The Billie Love Historical Collection 13, 15, 16, 20, 22, 29, 30, 31, 32, 33, 35, 37, 44, 45, 47 [top], 48, 53, 58, 59 [top and bottom], 60, 61, 62, 63, 64, 65 [top and bottom], 66, 67, 72 [top and bottom], 73 [top and bottom], 74, 100 [top]; The HSBC, Hongkong and Shanghai Banking Corporation Limited (Group Archives) 123; Interfoto-München, 18, 47 [bottom], 75 [bottom], 76, 86; The Mansell Collection 17, 97 [bottom], 98; The Mary Evans Picture Library 23; Mrs Hedda Morrison 101, 102 [top and bottom], 103 [bottom], 105 [middle], 106 [middle], 107 [bottom]; Oxford University Press 19, 21, 23, 24, 26, 27, 42, 52, 56, 136.

(Every effort has been made to trace copyright holders. We apologize for any errors or omissions in the above list and would be grateful to be notified of any corrections that should be incorporated in any future editions.)

I

Foreigners
in the
Middle Kingdom

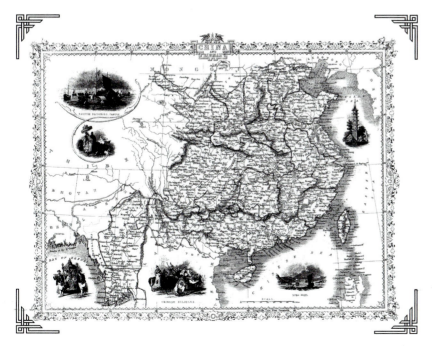

◄

*Map of China by
J. Rapkin from his*
Illustrated Atlas,
*published in London in
1851.*

IN THE EARLY hours of the morning, on Friday, 22 March 1861, two men departed on horseback from Tianjin for Peking. Several weeks before, an advance party, together with a long line of mule-drawn carts conveying personal baggage and other necessities had set out before them, accompanied by an escort of Sikh cavalry. Arriving in Peking on 26 March, the two riders took up residence in separate quarters prepared for them in advance in the southern corner of the Tartar City, not far from the Imperial Palace. On the top of one of the buildings the Tricolour was hoisted, and on the other the Union Jack was unfurled into the winds of Peking.

The two riders who arrived in Peking on that cold March day—Monsieur de Bourboulon and Mr (later Sir) Frederick Bruce, Ministers Extraordinaire of France and Great Britain, respectively—were not the first foreigners to have visited the Chinese capital. Nor were they the first to take up residence in the city.

Long before them, other visitors, including Marco Polo, Arab traders, and Indian Buddhist monks, had spent considerable periods of residence in Peking. Tribute bearers, arriving from Nepal, Annam, Korea, and elsewhere, made annual journeys to Peking where they bestowed gifts on the Emperor and traded in the city's markets. The Jesuits, during the seventeenth century, established a significant presence in Peking. For a time they enjoyed the patronage of the 'dragon throne' and enjoyed considerable influence and prestige at court.

But the visit of Monsieur de Bourboulon and Mr Bruce to Peking in 1861 was quite different from that of their predecessors. For they had come to China's capital not as private traders or missionaries or curious visitors. Rather, they came as representatives of their respective governments to establish permanent Legations in the Chinese capital. From these Legations they intended to interact directly with the Chinese authorities on matters relating to trade and other areas of common interest—not as vassals or tribute bearers, but as representatives of sovereign States with a status equal to that of China. It was something which was entirely without precedent.

The events of March 1861 marked a turning point in China's traditional pattern of relations with the outside world. For centuries, China—*Zhongguo*, or the 'Middle Kingdom'—had seen itself as being at the very centre of the universe—richer, more powerful, and culturally superior to all of its neighbours. China's

▲

View of the Great Wall from the outskirts of Peking, mid-1850s. Imperial China—the 'Middle Kingdom'—saw itself as the centre of the world with a culture superior to that of foreign 'barbarians'. The wall was a tangible manifestation of the Chinese sense of separateness.

relations with the 'barbarians' who lived along its periphery were conducted in accordance with a formal and structured ritual of obeisance known as the tribute system.

Under this system, which was in effect a substitute for familiar Western patterns of diplomacy and trade, foreign representatives were welcomed to the Middle Kingdom only as tributary vassals. As such, foreign representatives were expected to make periodic visits to the capital at Peking where they exchanged gifts with Chinese officials and performed the ritual of the *koutou* or 'kow-tow'—laying prostrate and making nine knocks of the head on the floor—before the 'Son of Heaven', or Emperor, and then returning to their home countries.

This traditional pattern of Chinese–foreign intercourse was a world apart from the concept of sovereign States dealing with each other on an equal footing which had been evolving in Europe over the preceding centuries. Under the Western system, the establishment of permanent representations in

3

foreign capitals had become an accepted custom, useful for the facilitation of trade and the conduct of political relations among nations. To the Chinese, however, the very concept was an affront to the view they held of the world and their place in it.

The Chinese had made known their views on the subject plainly enough in 1793. During that year Lord Macartney of Great Britain visited the Emperor's summer residence in Jehol. Macartney had been sent by the British government to negotiate a trade agreement with the Chinese and to obtain their permission for the delegation of a British minister to reside in Peking.

Lord Macartney arrived for his audience with the Emperor carrying several cases full of British manufactured goods intended as gifts for the Chinese sovereign. The gift-giving was calculated to whet the appetites of the Chinese for foreign goods and to convince them of the benefits of expanding foreign trade. The Emperor, however, was not impressed. Dismissing Lord Macartney's proposals, he said:

Our Celestial Empire possesses all things in prolific abundance, and lacks no product within its own borders. There is therefore no need to import the manufactures of outside barbarians in exchange for our own produce . . . As to your entreaty to send one of your nationals to be accredited to my Celestial Court, and to be in control of your country's trade with China, this request is contrary to all usages of my dynasty and cannot possibly be entertained.

The failure of Macartney's mission left the British unamused —and undaunted. They remained determined, as did the other European Powers, to force Peking to accept 'normal' standards of international relations.

Many reasons were advanced for Macartney's lack of success. The one most widely believed at the time was that put forward by two Dutchmen then working for the Dutch East Indies Company. These two men—Mr Van Braam and Mr Titsingh—had spent many years in the Far East. They argued that Macartney's mission was doomed to failure from the beginning. The reason: his ignorance of Chinese customs and, in particular, his refusal to perform the kow-tow before the Emperor.

Hoping to prove their point, and open up China's foreign trade to their own country ahead of the British, Van Braam and Titsingh visited Peking as envoys of the Dutch throne in 1795. As predicted, they were indeed required to perform the kow-tow as a condition to their audience before the Emperor Qian Long, and as promised, they did comply. Unfortunately, however, it is said that at the crucial moment in the ceremony Van Braam's wig fell off and the Emperor burst out laughing. The two Dutchmen were treated courteously, but were soon sent away.

The kow-tow also proved to be a problem for the Russians. Tsar Alexander I sent a mission to Peking in 1805 in an attempt to negotiate a trade treaty. However, this mission failed even before the Russian representative arrived at the Chinese capital. The Chinese advance party had insisted that the Russian representatives be prepared to kow-tow during their audience with the Emperor. They refused. After four months of negotiations, the Chinese invitation to visit Peking was withdrawn.

The British tried again in 1816. In that year, Lord Amherst was sent to Peking and arrived on 28 August. Once again, the kow-tow proved troublesome. Amherst had been told quite clearly by the Chinese that the kow-tow would be necessary if he were to meet with the Emperor. He replied that he would perform the ritual only if a Chinese Mandarin holding a rank equivalent to that of an English Lord would kow-tow before a portrait of the British Prince Regent. Needless to say, the Chinese did not agree. Serious discussions ensued, but no agreement was reached. At last, Amherst was informed that, under the circumstances, no audience would take place. Lord Amherst and his mission were ordered to depart the capital immediately.

Soon thereafter—as if in reaction to the inscrutable obstinacy of the foreign visitors—the Chinese Emperor issued an edict confirming the regulations previously put in place to govern China's trade with the foreigners and to restrict their activities largely to Canton. Under these rules, visits by foreigners to Peking would only be permitted on special occasions, and their period of residence in the Chinese capital could in no event exceed 46 days.

The 'Canton system', as the Chinese foreign trade regime was called, first came into being in 1760. Designed as a method to contain foreign influence in China while permitting regulated trade, the system restricted Chinese–foreign trade activity to one location, the southern-port city of Canton.

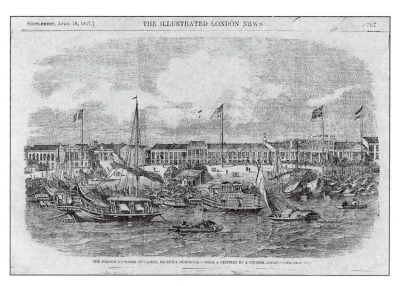

SUPPLEMENT, APRIL 18, 1857.]   THE ILLUSTRATED LONDON NEWS

THE FOREIGN FACTORIES AT CANTON, RECENTLY DESTROYED.—FROM A PAINTING BY A CHINESE ARTIST.—(SEE PAGE 371.)

The European Factories at Canton, from an early nineteenth-century engraving. The so-called 'factories' were, in fact, business agencies representing the commercial interests of over a dozen European and American companies. They were an integral part of the 'Canton system' of foreign trade regulation imposed by the Imperial Chinese Government on the West.

Foreign merchants were permitted to erect warehouses or 'factories' on a narrow strip of land measuring 1,100 by 700 feet along the Pearl River waterfront, but they were not allowed to travel inside the city itself without an official escort. Nor were they allowed to learn the Chinese language, or to bring their families to live with them in Canton. Indeed, Canton itself was only opened to foreign traders for limited periods between October to March each year. During the closed season, most foreign merchants lived with their families in nearby Macau, a settlement established earlier by the Portuguese, located down the Pearl River estuary along the coast.

To a very large extent, it was the Canton system and the other restrictions on trade imposed by the Chinese which prompted the early diplomatic visits to Peking. Only by establishing conventional relationships between the Chinese Emperor and foreign sovereigns, it was believed, would China then at last see the benefits of opening the country up to unrestricted, mutually beneficial trade. The kow-tow was only a symbol; the real problem was trade.

The trade issue became more urgent year after year as the balance of trade weighed heavily in China's favour. With soaring demand in Europe and the United States for Chinese silk and tea, the closed Chinese trading system limited the importation of American and European goods. As a result, the Western Powers strongly believed that Chinese impediments to free trade had to be done away with, to stem the flow of European cash into Chinese coffers.

The solution to these economic difficulties was not found in any voluntary relaxation of trade restrictions by the Chinese. Rather, the problem was solved by the creation of demand in China for a very special product—opium.

Labelled as 'happiness and longevity gum', or *fu-shou gao*, opium consumption was consciously promoted and encouraged by Western traders and their local Chinese business agents. So successful were these efforts that within a short time the popularity of opium among all strata of Chinese society became widespread. By the 1830s, demand for the drug had jumped to such alarming heights that the balance of trade had shifted in favour of the West. Moreover, the annual outflow of Chinese silver had begun to have a serious impact on the Chinese economy.

Once Peking had grasped the gravity of the situation, it determined to impose a full ban on the opium trade. An able official named Lin Zexu was put in charge of the task. After appealing to the British to take action voluntarily to end the opium trade, Lin issued an ultimatum prohibiting the importation of the drug into China. Soon thereafter, he discovered a large consignment of opium had just entered Canton. He ordered the cargo seized and destroyed.

The reaction among the foreign traders was one of outrage and indignation. Confrontation followed. Within a short time British warships arrived in China, followed by the landing of British troops. Offering little resistance, the Chinese Imperial Army forces sent to repel the 'foreign devils' were quickly defeated.

The result of this débâcle was the Treaty of Nanjing signed by China, under duress, in 1842. Under the terms of this treaty, a number of Chinese ports were opened to foreign trade and other concessions were granted. In addition, Hong Kong was ceded to Britain, missionaries were granted the right to preach within the treaty ports, an indemnity was imposed, and British nationals were granted extraterritorial rights in China. One point on which the Chinese successfully resisted British demands concerned the opening of China's capital to foreigners. Despite pressure from London, the Chinese refused to accept the establishment of foreign Legations in Peking.

The Emperor Daoguang reviewing his troops inside the Forbidden City in Peking, as depicted by a contemporary engraving. It was during the period of Daoguang's rule that China was forced to sign the Treaty of Nanjing in 1842. The treaty ended the first Opium War.

After the Treaty of Nanjing, Western powers became increasingly aggressive towards China. The next major confrontation occurred in 1856. After an incident involving an alleged Chinese attack on a small British vessel named the *Arrow*, war broke out once again. British forces began the action by attacking Canton. They were soon joined by the French. The city fell quickly after offering only scattered resistance.

Later, a naval task force was sent north to launch an attack against the Chinese forts at Dagu, which guarded the approach from the sea to Tianjin. At first, the Chinese called for a truce and proposed negotiations. When the British and French negotiators arrived, however, they were taken hostage by the Chinese. The British and French forces—joined later by Russians and Americans—then attacked Tianjin and occupied the city.

Led by Lord James Bruce, the Eighth Earl of Elgin (1811–63), the foreigners next turned their attention to the terms of the peace settlement which they would impose on the Chinese. Each of the allies who had participated in the attack negotiated separate agreements with the Chinese representatives. However, an identical clause was inserted in each peace treaty which granted to each Power 'most favoured nation' treatment. In layman's terms, this meant that each of the Powers could claim for itself the right to enjoy any benefit which China granted in its settlements to any of the other Powers.

HWA-SHA-NA.   THE EARL OF ELGIN.   KWEI-LIANG.   ADMIRAL SEYMOUR.

SIGNING OF THE TREATY BETWEEN ENGLAND AND CHINA AT TSIEN-TSIN ON JUNE 26, 1858.—SEE NEXT PAGE.

▲

This contemporary engraving depicts the signing of the Treaty of Tianjin by representatives of China and Great Britain on 26 June 1858. The European figure seated at the centre is Lord Elgin. The Treaty gave Great Britain the right to establish a permanent Legation in Peking.

The British signed their settlement—known as the Treaty of Tianjin—on 26 June 1858. The provisions included in the treaty were the same as those found in the settlements China reached with the other Powers but for one. Apart from securing Chinese agreement to the opening up of additional treaty ports and granting other trade concessions, the British treaty included a clause granting them the right to establish a Legation in Peking and to send an envoy to permanently reside there.

The 'Legation Clause' was not won easily. In the course of the treaty negotiations, the Chinese bitterly opposed the clause

9

and, at one point, went so far as to inform the British party that the Emperor had indicated that he would prefer a renewal of war to acceptance of the clause. The threat was dismissed by the British, and eventually the Chinese relented. Or at least so it seemed.

The treaty was signed, with the offending clause included, as scheduled. Yet, hardly was the ink dry when the Chinese renewed their attempts to strike the Legation Clause from the treaty. Failing this, they begged that the treaty be given a 'liberal interpretation' so that the establishment of a permanent Legation need not necessarily follow from the treaty's coming into force.

After much consideration, Lord Elgin, in what seems to have been a rare moment of sympathy for the Chinese, wrote a letter to the Chinese negotiators promising that:

If HM's Ambassador be properly received at Peking when the ratifications are exchanged next year, and full effect given in all other particulars to the treaty negotiated at Tientsin, it would certainly be expedient that HM's representative in China should be instructed to choose a place of residence elsewhere than at Peking, and to make his visits to the capital either periodical, or only as frequent as the exegesis of the public service may require.

The Chinese, having now obtained what was in effect a reprieve, proceeded directly to pursue a course of action which caused them to lose what they had won. The British Treaty of Tianjin, like the treaties with the other Western Powers, provided that instruments of ratification were to be exchanged by the Chinese and the foreigners in Peking within a year after the date of signing. Accordingly, Mr Bruce and Monsieur de Bourboulon arrived in Tianjin in 1859 with the intention to proceed to Peking for the ratifications. As it turned out, the Chinese refused them permission to make the journey. After they tried to force their way up the river from Tianjin the Chinese attacked their escorts, sinking four British gunboats.

Mr Bruce—who was, coincidentally, the brother of Lord Elgin—and Monsieur de Bourboulon, then returned to Tianjin. To their surprise, they then discovered that their American counterpart, Mr Ward, had been invited by the Chinese authorities to Peking via another route. However, he too met with difficulties. Upon his arrival in the capital on 28 July 1859,

Mr Ward found himself virtually a prisoner. Confined indoors, denied permission to ride or even walk about the city, Mr Ward described his party as being 'lodged in a well-furnished house and luxuriously fed, but . . . guarded like criminals'. Eventually, after some days of waiting, Ward was escorted out of the capital on 12 August.

The Chinese refusal to permit ratification of the treaties in Peking as previously agreed, enraged Lord Elgin and his allies. In 1860, they returned to China determined to force the Chinese to comply with their treaty obligations. The British came with 41 warships, 143 transport vessels, and more than 10,000 troops. The French contributed more than 6,000 soldiers who joined the British under Elgin's command. Launching a full attack on Peking, the city fell surprisingly quickly with little serious resistance from Imperial troops. Looting and wanton acts of violence by foreign troops then ensued, culminating in the destruction of the *Yuanming Yuan*, the Imperial Summer Palace designed by the Jesuits several centuries earlier. The Chinese were now humiliated and their troops broken. The Emperor fled the city to Jehol where he died soon afterwards. The government he left behind in Peking sued for peace.

On 24 October 1860, Lord Elgin entered Peking. Marching along streets lined by British troops, he proceeded to the *Li Bu* or Board of Rites. There the Convention of Peking was signed and instruments of ratification of the Treaty of Tianjin were exchanged. The Convention confirmed the provisions contained in the treaties of 1858, including the British Treaty of Tianjin. It also added a number of new provisions which substantially increased the price China was forced to pay for its resistance to the Western Powers.

Most importantly, the Convention of Peking abrogated the compromise regarding the 'Legation Clause' which Lord Elgin had made with the Chinese two years earlier. As a result, the right of the British to establish and maintain a permanent Legation in Peking was to be exercised forthwith. By virtue of the 'most favoured nation' clause, the same right was vested in the other treaty Powers. What China had long resisted, it was now compelled by force of arms to accept.

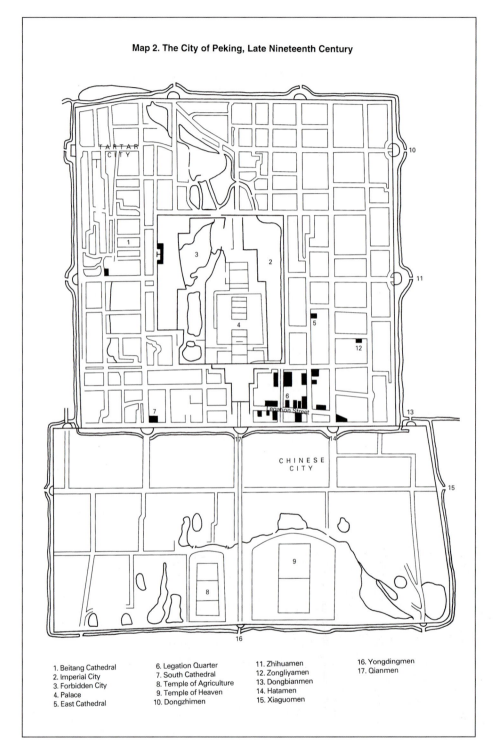

Map 2. The City of Peking, Late Nineteenth Century

1. Beitang Cathedral
2. Imperial City
3. Forbidden City
4. Palace
5. East Cathedral
6. Legation Quarter
7. South Cathedral
8. Temple of Agriculture
9. Temple of Heaven
10. Dongzhimen
11. Zhihuamen
12. Zongliyamen
13. Dongbianmen
14. Hatamen
15. Xiaguomen
16. Yongdingmen
17. Qianmen

II

The Early Legations

◀

The Dongjiaomin Xiang—*'Eastern Lane of the Mingling of Peoples'—dates from the Yuan dynasty when it was a major Customs entry point into Peking. Later, the district became a commercial centre and place of residence for foreign tribute bearers. After the Convention of Peking, the foreign Powers were permitted to establish Legations in the area and promptly renamed the main thoroughfare 'Legation Street'. This early photograph shows the intersection of Legation Street and the* Yühe *or Imperial Canal, a drainage ditch whose source was the Imperial Palace.*

AFTER THE ARRIVAL in Peking in March 1861 of the British and French envoys, Mr Bruce and Monsieur de Bourboulon, the other treaty Powers, Russia and the United States, began to make preparations to establish Legations of their own. The Russian envoy, General L. de Balluseck, arrived in Peking on 8 July. The United States sent its envoy, Mr Anson Burlingame, in the autumn of 1861. However, after spending time in Canton and Shanghai, he did not reach Peking until 20 July 1862.

In the meantime, other countries had begun to pressure China to grant to them the same rights conceded to the original four treaty Powers. The first to raise a vigorous claim against China was Prussia. On 23 June 1861 Prussia's envoy, Graf Eulenburg, arrived in Tianjin and opened negotiations with the Chinese. The talks progressed in a serpentine manner, and it soon became apparent that the Chinese were intent on delaying the discussions. At this point Eulenburg seized the initiative and dispatched two members of his staff to Peking to prepare for the establishment of a Legation, with or without the consent of the Chinese. This move, accompanied by ominous threats of Prussian military action, persuaded the Chinese to adopt a more compliant negotiating stance.

After further protracted negotiations, a treaty was signed on 2 September 1861. As a result of this treaty, Prussia, both on her own behalf and on behalf of the other members of the German Zoll-und-Handelsverein, obtained from the Chinese commercial and extraterritorial rights of much the same kind as had been granted to the four Western signatories of the Tianjin treaties of 1858. However, as might have been expected, the Chinese balked at the Prussian demand for the establishment of a Legation in Peking.

The issue was finally resolved in characteristic Chinese manner, namely by a 'mutual accommodation'. In brief, China agreed to grant Prussia the right to send its envoy to reside permanently in Peking, but Prussia agreed to defer the exercise of its right for a period of five years. As a result, Eulenburg ordered his aides to withdraw from Peking where they had set up quarters next door to the British. The first official Prussian envoy arrived in the capital in 1866.

Following Prussia's example, other Western Powers commenced negotiations in due course to establish trade relations with China along the lines laid down in the Tianjin treaties. Among the benefits which these countries sought was the right to establish a permanent Legation in Peking. By the end of the nineteenth century, foreign pressure on China resulted in the establishment of eleven Legations in the Chinese capital, including those of Austria–Hungary, Belgium, Great Britain, France, Germany, Holland, Italy, Japan, Russia, Spain, and the United States.

When the representatives of the original four treaty Powers first arrived in Peking in the early 1860s, the Chinese proposed that their Legations be established at the site of the old Imperial Summer Palace—the *Yuanming Yuan*—which had been destroyed by foreign troops during the battles which preceded the signing of the Convention of Peking. The foreign envoys, however, viewed this proposal as yet another attempt to keep the foreigners and their Legations at a distance, outside the confines of Peking proper. Accordingly, the proposal was rejected, and the Chinese were forced to come up with another site.

The district which later became the Legation Quarter was located along the inside of the Tartar Wall between the Qianmen to the east and the Hatamen to the west. In this early photograph the Legations are situated to the right of the wall.
▼

The location which the Chinese next proposed was an area of the city to the eastern side of the Qianmen Gate along the southern wall of the Tartar City. To Chinese residents, the

15

area was known by the name of the main thoroughfare—
Dongjiaomin Xiang or 'Eastern Lane of the Mingling of
Peoples'—which cut through the district and ran parallel to
the city wall between the Qianmen Gate on the west and the
Hatamen Gate on the east.

The existence of the *Dongjiaomin Xiang* dates back to the
days of the Mongol or Yuan Dynasty in the fourteenth century AD. At that time, the street was called *Jiangmi Xiang*, or
'Glutinous Rice Lane', because it constituted the main entrance
point into the capital for rice and other goods shipped from
the south. It was also the place where traders visiting the capital from other parts of China gathered and stayed. Because
of its importance as a commercial centre, an Imperial Customs
Station was built on the site.

In the later dynasties, the association of the district with
people and things foreign endured. For example, it was here
that the Chinese authorities established the *Siyiguan* or 'Four
Barbarians Hostel' which housed representatives from the tribute kingdoms of Annam, Burma, Korea, and Mongolia when
they visited Peking on their annual rite of obeisance to the
Emperor. Certainly, the history of the district, and its associ-
ations with visiting 'barbarians' and tribute rituals, could not
have been unknown to the Chinese officials who proposed
it as the place for the establishment of the early Legations.
However, the significance which the area held for the Chinese
was in all likelihood lost on the first foreign envoys. For them,
the proposal that they be allocated an area inside the city
walls not far from the Imperial Palace itself was nothing short
of a victory, and they accepted it gladly.

The Tartar Wall in the late 1800s.
The Legation Quarter sat directly
behind the wall. The Qianmen is
visible in the distance.

Over the next decades the basic outlines of what ultimately became known as the Legation Quarter began to take shape. The area was bounded on the south by the Tartar City Wall which stretched along for about one mile between the Qianmen and the Hatamen, two of the city's largest gates. The wall itself was massive: 44 feet (15 metres) high, 62 feet (21 metres) thick at the bottom, and 34 feet (11 metres) thick at the top. To the north the crimson walls of the Imperial City defined the outer reaches of the community. The eastern boundary was formed by Hatamen Street which stretched from the south to the great Changan Avenue in the north. The western limits were a series of Chinese government buildings and ministries.

Running from north to south close to the middle of this rectangular district was the Imperial Canal, or *Yühe*. Actually little more than a muddy ditch, the source of the canal's slow-running water was said to be the three 'seas' or lakes within the Imperial Palace grounds. Because of its foul smell, many early foreign residents of the Legation Quarter assumed the canal's 'water' was in reality sewage from the Imperial Palace directed—by design—into the very centre of the foreign community. In the 1800s the canal was crossed by three bridges. The first bridge lay outside the Quarter to the north. The second spanned the canal at the *Dongjiaomin Xiang*, now renamed Legation Street. The third bridge made its crossing at the edge of the Tartar City Wall to the south. As the canal crossed under the southern bridge it wandered under and through the city wall via a tunnel which could be shut by a wooden gate, known as the Water Gate (*Shuiguan*).

This early photograph provides a view from the intersection of Legation Street and the Imperial Canal looking northwards. The Western-style building on the left is the British Legation. The Legation's main gate had not yet been built.

▼

Not all foreigners in Peking resided within the general bounds of the Legation Quarter. A number of foreign institutions—especially churches and missionary establishments—were located beyond the confines of the *Dongjiaomin Xiang*. These included Matteo Ricci's Southern Cathedral, or *Nantang*, as well as the Jesuits' earlier headquarters at the *Beitang*, or Northern Cathedral. The Anglican Mission Society's headquarters, as well as those of the London Mission and the American Presbyterian and Methodist Missions, were all set up at some distance away from Legation Street. In fact, during the nineteenth century the general area popularly described as the 'Legation Quarter' was neither defined by law nor reserved exclusively for residence by foreigners. No walls were erected to keep the foreigners in or to push the Chinese out. Indeed, up until 1900 the Legation community was, in physical terms at least, intermixed with the Chinese community. The Western-style villas and renovated Chinese structures which became the Legations sat side-by-side with the more modest dwellings of ordinary Chinese and the offices of various Chinese government departments.

Prior to the Boxer Siege in 1900, most of the foreign Legations lay scattered among Chinese dwellings and official government offices. This photograph, probably from the 1870s, shows Chinese residents of the district walking towards Legation Street. The British Legation is visible in the background.

▼

Within the Quarter, Legation Street was the main thoroughfare, and from it branched off numerous smaller roads which marked out the edges of the *hutong*—the traditional neighbourhoods whose small alleyways provided access into and out of Peking's walled residential compounds. During most of the nineteenth century, Legation Street—along with smaller by-passes—was left unpaved and pocked with holes and ruts. Depending on the season the roads were either clogged with mud and water or gave up great clouds of dust whenever a donkey carriage or sedan-chair passed by.

Map 1 (set out on the front endpapers of the book) provides a general idea of the layout of the Legation Quarter in the nineteenth century. At the western end of the Quarter, Bingbu Street stretched from north to south. As the entrance ways to several important government departments opened out onto this street, gates were built at each end and these were opened at dawn and were closed shut in the evening. The main departments located along Bingbu Street were the Board of War, the Board of Works, the Board of State Ceremonies, the Board of Astronomy, and the Board of Medicine.

A Chinese resident looks down upon the Legation Quarter from a position on top of the Tartar City Wall. The building in the background appears to belong to the old American Legation prior to its destruction during the Boxer Siege of 1900.

Running parallel to Bingbu Street to the west was Hubu Street. Along this street were the following government departments: the Prefecture of Imperial Clan Affairs, the Board of Civil Affairs, the Board of Revenue, and the Board of Rites. The latter building served as the venue for the signing of the Convention of Peking in 1860 between Prince Kung and the British and French envoys, Lord Elgin and

Baron Gros. The main gates of the four departments all faced Hubu Street.

At the eastern side of the Board of War was the Imperial Carriage House. This building was used as a garage for the many carriages, sedan chairs and carts which were used by the Emperor during imperial ceremonies. The park which surrounded the Carriage House included several stables where elephants, who were often called into service to pull the carriages, were housed. Most of the elephants were presented as tribute gifts to the Emperor by the sovereigns of Annam and Nepal.

South-east of the Board of Works was an unoccupied plant used as a factory for construction materials. North-east of the Carriage House was the Imperial Academy. Its main gate faced Changan Avenue. The Imperial Academy, or *Hanlin Yuan*, consisted of a large garden which contained between 20 to 25 separate halls constructed in the traditional Chinese style. The Academy was founded in 1740 and functioned as a kind of national library and research academy for the literary elite. Among its many treasures was the Yung Lo Encyclopaedia which consisted of nearly 23,000 volumes.

The British established their Legation in the former palace of the Duke of Liang. The premises were initially leased from the Liang household at an annual rent of £500. The rent was paid each year by delivery of the precise amount in silver ingots. A special silk top hat was reserved for use by the Legation official assigned the task of delivering the rent on behalf of Her Majesty's Government in the late 1800s. This photograph from the late 1890s shows the traditional Chinese gardens which were preserved by the British inside their Legation compound.

South of the Imperial Academy was the British Legation. The British, being among the earliest to take up premises in the Quarter, were able to secure the largest piece of land for their Legation. The site, which included a *wangfu* or palace, and numerous other buildings, originally belonged to one of the 33 sons of the Emperor Kangxi who himself had received it as a gift from his father. When Kangxi's son died, the property was passed on to his various male descendants who bore the title 'Duke of Liang'. By 1860, when the British arrived, the palace buildings and grounds were badly in need of repair. Extensive renovations were made to render the buildings habitable, but the traditional Chinese style of the construction was maintained.

Under the terms of its occupancy grant, the British Government leased the palace—or *fu* as it came to be called—and the surrounding grounds in perpetuity, at a rent of about £500 per annum. Until the Siege in 1900, the British Legation faithfully paid the rent on schedule, loading a special cart with silver ingots every Chinese New Year and delivering the rent to the Zongli Yamen, or foreign office. The British official accompanying the cart was, by tradition, the Chinese Secretary of the Legation—usually a British student of the Chinese language preparing for service in the Imperial Maritime Customs. In a typically British approach to such matters, the Legation reportedly reserved a special silk top-hat for use on this annual occasion.

In late 1861 the British Legation expanded its site to include the adjacent piece of land to the north. This parcel was first occupied by the Prussian representatives who arrived earlier in 1861 and then departed after the signing of the Prussian Treaty in Tianjin. The British then purchased the site and rented it to the Lockhart Mission Hospital. When the hospital later moved to a different location near Hatamen Street, the site was formally incorporated into the British Legation compound.

Wedged in between the British Legation and Chinese government department offices was an open space known as the Mongol Quarter. This area was the site of a fair held throughout the winter by Mongols who came down from the steppes to trade. The visitors pitched their tents in the area and conducted business in the midst of the camels, the cooking fires, and the Chinese traders who wandered amongst them.

▲
The British retained many of the old Chinese-style buildings inside their Legation. Although a two-storeyed Western building was constructed for use as a chancery, most of the residential buildings used by British Legation officials were the original structures from the Liang Palace. The photograph shows the classical Chinese interior of the British Legation in the late 1890s.

South of the Mongol Quarter was the Russian Legation. Its main gate facing out onto Legation Street, the Russian Legation was in fact the oldest foreign-owned site in the Quarter. Under the terms of the Kiakhta Treaty entered into between Russia and China in 1727, the Emperor granted the right of residence in Peking to a small group of Russian Orthodox priests and Chinese-language students. The group was given a small plot of land on which were built a residence and a chapel.

The origin of this foreign presence in the Chinese capital dates back to a curious incident which occurred in 1685, during the reign of Peter the Great. At that time, fighting had broken out along the Chinese border between Chinese settlers and a group of Russians known as Albazines. During years of protracted strife, a number of Russian prisoners were taken by the Chinese and sent to Peking.

22

When the fighting ceased, the Russian captives in Peking were offered residence in the capital. Most accepted, and many of the Russians later intermarried with Peking residents. Over time they and their children became indistinguishable from the Chinese except for their Russian Orthodox religion to which they remained unswervingly loyal. After numerous petitions to the Chinese Emperor, he finally acceded to their request that a Russian ecclesiastical mission be permitted to reside in Peking to serve the spiritual needs of the Orthodox community.

Most of the Legations were clustered about Legation Street, as shown in this photograph from the late 1890s.

After the Treaty of Tianjin of 1858, the four Russian priests and six language students then resident in the mission were moved to other quarters, and the Russian Legation was established in their compound. As time went by, the Legation authorities gradually tore down the old mission buildings, many of which dated back to the 1700s, and built new ones. However, the small Russian Orthodox chapel and cemetery inside the old compound were maintained. Until its destruction in late 1991 to make way for a new building of the Chinese Supreme People's Court, the chapel was believed to be the oldest existing Western building in Peking.

Moving from west to east along Legation Street, the Dutch Legation and the American Legation lay to the right-hand side. The Dutch Legation sat between Legation Street and the Tartar City Wall. Located at the far end of the Quarter, it was surrounded by Chinese residences and government offices, and a Chinese temple to the God of Fire. (The Chinese incense burners which even today are to be found inside the grounds of the Dutch Legation probably originate from this temple.)

23

▲

The German Legation was first established on the south side of Legation Street opposite the French Legation. The building's plain front hid from view the many Western-style buildings which were constructed behind the Legation's walls.

The American Legation sat directly across Legation Street from the Russian Legation and was built on the original site of the 'Hostel of Tributary Nations'. The site consisted of about one acre over which was scattered various houses built in the Chinese style. The property was originally purchased by Dr S.S. Williams, the author of a Chinese–English Dictionary and a well-known, eighteenth-century description of China entitled *The Middle Kingdom*. Dr Williams leased the premises to the US Government until his death, after which the arrangement was continued by his heirs.

On the other side of the Imperial Canal, to the north, lay a large walled compound known as the *Suwangfu*, or residence of Prince Su, a Manchu noble. Within the compound, there were five separate arrangements of pavilions, artificial hills, and ponds all surrounding a main residence constructed in traditional Chinese style.

Along Legation Street, moving eastwards from the Canal, lay the Spanish Legation, the Japanese Legation, and the French Legation. On the opposite side of Legation Street was the German Legation.

24

The French established their Legation at about the same time as the British. Like the British Legation, the French site originally belonged to a Manchu noble who held the title Duke of Qin. By the mid-1800s the family had become impoverished and was happy to rent the dilapidated premises to the newly-arrived French. The French tore down most of the old palace buildings and constructed new quarters in the European style. Apart from its beautiful garden, the Legation was known for the two white stone lions which guarded its main gate.

The eastern end of the French Legation bordered on a long thoroughfare which ran parallel to the Imperial Canal from the Tartar Wall at the south to the Changan Avenue in the north. The street's original Chinese name was *Taijichang*—so called because it once served as the site of a large factory for drying wood used for fuel. By the 1870s it came to be known as 'Customs Street'. Later, as French influence in this part of the Quarter grew, French map-makers and francophones in the community began to refer to it as 'Rue Marco Polo'.

The origin of the name Customs Street relates to the establishment in 1865 on the eastern end of the street of the headquarters of the Inspectorate General of the Chinese Imperial Maritime Customs Service. Technically an agency of the Chinese Government, the Maritime Customs was in fact a semi-autonomous organization created and run by foreigners whose primary task was to enforce a uniform tariff in China's international trade. Although the revenues collected by the Maritime Customs were nominally the property of the Chinese Government, by the late 1800s most had been pledged to the service of China's foreign debt.

The area opposite the Customs compound, lying between Customs Street and Hatamen Street, was crowded with the residences of ordinary Peking citizens. Only two Legations were established here. In the north-west corner of the area was the Legation of Austria–Hungary, built in 1871. To the south, along Legation Street, was the Italian Legation, established in the 1870s.

The only Legation which was established outside the Quarter was that of the Belgians. For reasons still unclear, the Belgians constructed their Legation on the eastern side of Hatamen Street beyond the Changan Avenue to the north, some distance from Legation Street where most of the Legation compounds were clustered. It would prove to be a fatal mistake.

Hatamen Street, today's Chongwenmen Dajie, formed the eastern boundary of the general area which came to be known as the Legation Quarter. At the south, the district was entered from the Hatamen Gate, shown here from the outside. The Legations were clustered inside, through the gate to the left.

For in the 'Boxer troubles' of 1900, the Belgian Legation was among the first to be attacked.

Now that we have seen how the early Legations came to be, and where they were first established, we turn to look at what life was like in the Chinese capital in the nineteenth century and how the foreign community related to the Chinese inhabitants of Peking.

III

Peking and the Foreign Community in the Nineteenth Century

◄

Nineteenth-century Peking was a romantic, but not particularly desirable, posting for foreign diplomats. The city's walls and palaces were poorly maintained and the standard of living of its inhabitants was low compared with that of London or Paris. Camel caravans were the lifeblood of the Chinese capital's trade and transportation system.

IN THE LATTER half of the nineteenth century, Peking was not viewed by foreign diplomats as a particularly desirable posting. Although the romance of the 'Middle Kingdom' still held a special allure for Westerners, everyday life in the Chinese capital outside the gates of the Legations was filled with sundry unpleasant adversities.

The first of the many hardships encountered by foreigners sent to take up residence in Peking was the arduous task of getting there. After a long sea journey, travellers disembarked at the northern Chinese coastal city of Tianjin. Following a brief rest, Peking-bound foreigners had a choice of two different routes—by land across 80 miles of dusty plains or by boat up the Beihe River to the town of Tongzhou which lay 14 miles from Peking's city walls. For travellers in a hurry, the land route was preferred. After arranging for several ponies, a wagon to carry the luggage, and a *mafu* or Chinese groom, the traveller and his entourage would leave at daybreak the following morning. If the weather was good, the group could easily make 40 miles in a day and would spend the night at a Chinese inn. The group would have to be up again and on the road several hours before dawn so as to reach Peking before the city gates were closed in the evening.

The journey by land might be considerably longer if women and children were among the party. In such a case, ponies would normally be abandoned in favour of the Peking cart. The discomfort which passengers had to endure by choosing this mode of transport must have made the journey seem even longer than it was. One traveller in the late 1800s described a journey in the Peking cart in the following terms:

[The cart is] an enormously strong and heavy square two-wheeled, covered vehicle, drawn by a mule, the passenger squatting tailor-fashion inside and the driver sitting on the shaft . . . to be rolled about and jolted in one of these is simple torture, and if you do not hold on closely to the hand-rails inside you run no little risk of having your brains dashed out.

Travel from Tianjin to Peking by boat not only took longer, between three to six days, but was also more expensive. Still, until the railway line was connected between Tianjin and Peking in the 1890s, travel by house boat towed by a steam tug was considered the most comfortable way to make the

▲

The infamous Peking cart was reviled by foreigners but was the main mode of transport in northern China in the nineteenth century. It was extremely uncomfortable to ride in because it had no springs. The many ruts and holes in Peking's roads ensured a bumpy ride for any passenger.

journey. All in all, the trip from Tianjin to Tongzhou along the winding river covered a distance of 120 miles. At Tongzhou, passengers were discharged and transferred to Peking carts or sedan chairs for the final 14-mile journey to Peking.

The sight of the Peking city walls from a distance has been described by a number of contemporary travellers as a moment of intense excitement. However, the vision of Peking which foreigners carried in their imaginations often failed to coincide with reality. Henry Norman, a traveller writing in the 1890s, described his arrival in Peking thus:

You enter through a gate of no proportions or pretentions, you ride for a quarter of an hour among hovels and pigs, and then suddenly on climbing a bank a striking sight bursts upon you. A great tower of many storeys forms the corner of a mighty wall; from each of its storeys a score of cannon-mouths yawn; for a mile or more the wall stretches in a perfectly straight line, pierced with a thousand embrasures, supported by a hundred buttresses. Then you halt your pony and sit and try to realize that another of the desires of your life is

29

gratified; that you are at last really and truly before the walls of the city that was old centuries before the wolf and the woodpecker found Romulus and Remus; in the wonderland of Marco Polo, father of travellers; on the eve of exploring the very capital and heart of the Celestial Empire. This is the first of your two precious moments. When you ride on you discover that the cannon-mouths are just black and white rings painted on boards, and the swindle—fortunately you do not know it then—is your whole visit to Peking in a nutshell. The place is a gigantic disappointment . . . .The truth is that Peking is not worth the trip.

A view of the Peking city wall in the late 1890s.

The writer went on to note that the second of his 'two precious moments' was when the visitor was at last able to leave Peking.

For many Europeans, a major source of disappointment was the discovery that nineteenth-century Peking was singularly unattractive. The streets were laid out at right angles in a checkerboard plan of what seemed to be unrelenting monotony. The only exceptions were the narrow, dark alleyways which cut across and through the *hutong*. The roads themselves were uneven, unpaved, and riddled with holes. In the rainy season they were little more than mud ditches and were all but impassable.

By the mid-1800s the glory of Peking's traditional architecture was in a state of widespread disrepair. Many of the temples and palace buildings were closed to the public, and those that were open were either broken down, poorly maintained, or wholly dilapidated.

30

▲

Peking's unpaved roads turned into muddy ditches during the rainy season and threw up swirls of dust during the dry, hot summer. This photograph, probably from the late 1880s, shows what is believed to be the Taijichang, later known as Customs Street or Rue Marco Polo.

Another unattractive feature was the Peking weather. While the autumn months were marked by clear skies and sunny days, the rest of the year was uncomfortable. In winter, the winds from the north were bitterly cold and the city was often immobilized by snow and ice. Spring brought sandstorms from the desert north. In summer the dry unrelenting heat, broken only by brief showers, parched the city and surrounding countryside.

The sanitary habits of Peking residents were another frequent source of complaint by foreigners. The habits of the native Pekingese were frequently described by foreigners as 'vile', the streets little more than 'public latrines'. Henry Norman described his impressions of Peking in the following vivid terms:

31

A Chinese market scene inside the Tartar City during the nineteenth century. Foreign residents of Peking during this period looked with disdain on the sanitary habits of ordinary Chinese.

Above all other characteristics of Peking one thing stands out in horrible prominence. Not to mention it would be willfully to omit the most striking feature of the place. I mean its filth. It is the most horribly and indescribably filthy place that can be imagined. Indeed, imagination must fall far short of the fact. Some of the daily sights of the pedestrians in Peking could hardly be more than hinted at by one man to another in the disinfecting atmosphere of a smoking-room. There is no sewer or cesspool, public or private, but the street; the dog, the pig, and the fowl—in sickening succession—are the scavengers; every now and then you pass a man who goes along tossing the most loathsome of refuse into an open-work basket on his back; the smells are simply awful; the city is one colossal and uncleansed *cloaca*.

Because the early Legations were established in the midst of the Chinese community, the characteristic features of old Peking were never far away. Norman, for example, described Legation Street as follows:

It is half a mile long, either mud or dust, as level as a chopping sea, with here and there its monotony of blank walls or dirty native

32

houses broken by a strong gateway with a couple of stone lions in front . . . . When your guide says, 'This is Legation Street,' you laugh, it is so dirty, so miserable, with its horrible crowd of dogs and pigs and filthy children. But when you have lived in it for a few days you laugh no more: you count the hours till you can get away.

Living as they were amongst ordinary Chinese, their Legations set alongside Chinese government offices and lowly residences, foreigners in the early Legation Quarter had ample opportunity to interact with Chinese citizens and vice versa. Unfortunately, it appears that physical proximity did not bring with it either familiarity or mutual respect.

Frequently referred to as *guizi* ('devils') or *maozi* ('hairy ones'), it is not surprising that foreigners felt that the Chinese despised them. Norman's description of an encounter with a group of curious Chinese while on a walkabout in Peking highlights the cultural gulf which separated the two communities during the early Legation years:

Prior to 1900 the foreign community of the Legations lived side-by-side with ordinary Peking residents. Physical proximity did not, however, always produce mutual affection or respect. Many Chinese referred to foreigners as 'devils' and most foreigners avoided social contacts with Peking residents outside official channels. This photograph shows a bustling street scene not far from the Legation Quarter in the late 1800s.

▼

They crowd round you whenever you stop and in a minute you are the centre of a mass of solid humanity, which is eating horrible stuff, which is covered with vermin, which smells worse than words can tell, and which is quite likely to have smallpox . . . .The crowd jostles you, feels your clothes with its dirty hands, pokes its nose in your face, keeping up all the time . . . a string of insulting and obscene remarks with accompanying roars of laughter.

As to relations with Chinese officials, one British Legation Offical summed up the commonly held view of most residents thus: 'The more they know us, the less they like us.' Although it appears there were occasions on which lower-ranked officials met socially with foreigners—especially, apparently, for card-playing—such informal mixing was discouraged by the Imperial Court.

The social distance maintained by many Chinese as a result of official policy and popular antipathy for foreigners was for the most part welcomed by foreign residents. Indeed, foreigners apparently felt as uneasy with the Chinese as the Chinese did with them. Charles Denby, long-serving Chief Minister of the American Legation, described the situation in 1885 in his memoirs:

Arriving at Peking, the first duty of the diplomatic stranger is to call on the Tsung-li Yamen, foreign office, to pay his respects and be recognized in his official capacity . . . .The call on the Yamen is the only one the stranger is required to make. In other countries official calls are the dread of the visitor, but there was in my day no court circle at Peking, and social intercourse with the foreigners was

Chinese officials maintained contact with the Legations through the Zongli Yamen, a government department which combined the functions of the Foreign Office and the Ministry of War. The Yamen's headquarters were located not far from the Legation Quarter. This photograph from about 1898 shows the entrance to the Yamen.

frowned on by the empress . . . .The absence of the necessity of meeting each other socially was a great relief both to the Chinese and to the foreigners. Except on rare occasions, social intercourse would have been exceedingly tedious for both parties.

Still, good relations with Chinese officials were crucial to the safety of the foreign community. As one diplomat in Peking remarked to a foreign visitor in the early 1890s:

If the Tsungli Yamen were abolished, our lives would not be safe here for twenty-four hours. The people just refrain from actually molesting us because they have learned that they will be very severely punished if they do.

Chinese officials travelled in style. This large sedan-chair is parked outside the British Legation alongside the Imperial Canal. Its owner was probably an official of the Zongli Yamen on a formal visit to HM's Minister in Peking.

▼

Faced with the 'difficult conditions' of life in the Middle Kingdom, the foreign residents of China's capital insulated themselves from the world outside by creating their own society with its own comforts, rules, and amusements.

By the end of the nineteenth century, the foreign population in Peking numbered about 500. Nearly half of these residents were either attached to one of the Legations or were proprietors or employees of one of the foreign-run establishments which served the Legation community. The remaining foreigners were members of one of the many missionary societies which had been established in the capital. Living in the mission stations scattered throughout Peking, the missionary community appears to have only rarely interacted with the 'official' foreign community largely clustered in the vicinity of Legation Street.

The diplomatic community, which consisted of the Legation diplomats and their families and assistants, has been described by contemporary writers as the 'life, soul and heart of the Peking foreign community' in the nineteenth century. Between themselves, they treated each other as 'one family'. The American Minister in Peking, Mr Charles Denby, described what this meant:

When a member [of the Diplomatic Corps] arrives at a post he must make the first call on all the other members, down to the wife of the youngest attaché. This duty performed, he and his family are received in friendly and even affectionate intercourse.

According to Denby, incidents of ill-will among members of the Diplomatic Corps were rare. That this was so was probably due to the fact that relations between the members of the community were regulated by a strict adherence to etiquette and propriety. Rank, in particular, was something of great concern to members of the diplomatic corps. The longest-serving diplomat then in Peking was known as 'the Doyen'. He not only convened the periodic plenary meetings of ministers, but was given the place of honour at every social function. The ranking of other ministers followed in accordance with the same rule: the longer the stay, the higher the status.

Life among the diplomats in the Quarter has been described as an 'endless round of balls, picnics and theatricals'. The British Legation was known for hosting the best dinner parties. Its dining room, with English crystal and silver service of

▲

Foreign residents of the Legations created their own Western life-style in the midst of Peking. This rare photograph shows the dining room of the British Legation before the Siege in the summer of 1900.

the highest quality, was said to have been the envy of many Legation wives. The Legation Quarter also supported two clubs. The French had their own club, whose membership was restricted to French nationals and other francophones. The larger club was the Peking Club which sat directly behind the German Legation. In the early 1890s, the Peking Club had about 40 members and included facilities such as a tennis court, a billiard room, a reading room, and card tables.

The Legation community supported two stores—Imbeck's next to the American Legation, and Kierulff's opposite the Spanish Legation—and several small hotels. The most popular was the original Hôtel de Pékin, run by a Swiss named Auguste Chamot and his American wife. The hotel's restaurant was said to be popular among Legation residents, and the Chamot couple were reputedly excellent cooks.

37

Because the Legation Quarter was not intended to be a trading centre as such, foreign businesses did not begin to establish a presence in the capital until the latter part of the nineteenth century. Among the first to set up offices in the Quarter were the traders Jardine, Matheson & Co. and several banks, including the Hongkong and Shanghai Bank.

The Legation community, despite the restrictions imposed by Peking, was in fact quite cosmopolitan. Most members had been posted previously in some of the world's largest cities and were fluent in a number of foreign languages. Within the Quarter itself, both English and French were widely used. Newspapers arrived (if quite late) from around the world, and a number of learned societies were organized, such as the Peking Branch of the Oriental Society of London.

Although foreigners within the Quarter appear to have clung closely to their own society, the Chinese world was never far away. Still, by the end of the nineteenth century, it appears that many foreign residents had come to believe that Chinese hostility toward the 'devils' and their Legations had subsided. As Arnot Reid, an English visitor to Peking in the early 1890s noted:

When I was in Peking the foreigner alone in the Peking streets at nightfall was as safe as he would be in Piccadilly, and a great deal safer than he would be in some districts of London . . . .The town was considered to be perfectly safe; and it was safe. The feeling of the people was supposed to be quite friendly; and it was friendly. Foreigners moved about with all the ease, freedom and safety with which they might move in their own native streets.

Had the Chinese at last come to accept the presence of foreigners within the gates of their capital? Or was the Londoner quoted above simply naïve? By the end of the nineteenth century the answer was clear. The true feelings of many Chinese were not at all friendly. Nor were the Legations safe.

▲

The foreign presence in Peking had become well-established by the end of the nineteenth century. Foreigners travelled freely throughout the city and its environs and few ever felt in danger. By the spring of 1900, however, anti-foreign hostility, which had long simmered below the surface, erupted. The subsequent attacks on the Legations nearly destroyed the community.

IV

The Siege of the Legations

The Siege of 1900 was led by the 'Boxers'—members of the 'Society of Righteous and Harmonious Fists'—an anti-foreign secret society which was made up mostly of peasants. This photograph shows members of a Boxer band in full garb.

DURING THE SUMMER months of 1900, armed Chinese launched a series of brutal attacks against the foreign community in Peking. By the time the foreigners were rescued, much of the old Legations lay in waste, the Empress Dowager had fled the capital, and Peking was once again occupied by foreign soldiers.

The Siege—as the attacks of June–August 1900 came to be known—was one of the most dramatic events in the history of modern Chinese–foreign relations. It also marked a turning point in the history of the Legation Quarter. For the assault on the beleaguered foreigners set in motion a chain of events which ultimately transformed the small foreign community clustered around the old *Dongjiaomin Xiang* into a walled foreign city, complete with its own troops, administration, and services, largely divorced from the Chinese world which surrounded it.

The Siege was, in truth, but one in a series of violent popular outbursts which swept China in the last years of the nineteenth century. The main causes of this unrest were a revival of Chinese xenophobia in the face of growing Western influence and aggression, a growing anti-dynastic sentiment, and severe economic hardship in the Chinese countryside.

Anti-foreign feeling was one of the driving forces behind the outbreak of the 'Boxer Troubles'. This poster from 1900 shows China under attack by eight different uniformed soldiers. They were presumably intended to represent the eight major Powers of the period—the United Kingdom, France, Russia, Belgium, the Netherlands, Italy, the United States, and Japan.

▼

In the years following the Treaty of Tianjin in 1858, foreign encroachments upon Chinese territory and sovereignty—perpetrated in the name of 'free trade' and 'Christianity and civilization'—continued unabated. The pattern of aggression was largely the same: foreigners pressed for their 'rights', the Chinese resisted, and the foreigners demanded, threatened, and pushed through the door. The results were enshrined in a number of treaties which, even today, the Chinese remember as fundamentally unequal. By the end of the nineteenth century, therefore, China had lost effective sovereignty over much of its territory. The country was a patchwork of foreign 'treaty ports', 'concession' areas, 'leased' cities, 'ceded' territories, and demarcated 'spheres of influence'. The once-proud Middle Kingdom which had struggled for so long to keep the foreign barbarians at a distance was now forced to live with them in its midst.

One of the most visible representations of the foreign presence in China was the missionary. After the Treaty of Nanjing in 1842, which legalized foreign religious activity in China, there began an aggressive missionary effort from both Europe and the United States 'to bring the word of Christ to the heathen Chinese'. Within a short period, missionary establishments had sprung up in cities, towns, and smaller villages throughout the country, making their presence felt in the everyday lives of ordinary Chinese. Although foreign missionaries were driven by lofty motives and their contributions to the welfare of ordinary Chinese were often real, their presence led overall to an increase in anti-foreign sentiment in China. Molded as they were by nineteenth-century Victorian values and convinced of the superiority of 'white, Western, Christian culture', many missionaries looked upon Chinese traditional values and customs with scant tolerance.

The tension which arose as a result of the clash of cultures between the Chinese and Western missionaries is dramatically illustrated by the debates which ensued during the late nineteenth century over Christian architecture in China. After the establishment of a missionary centre, one of the ambitions of all missionary groups was to erect a church. Usually built in the Western design with a high steeple or spire, the churches clashed with traditional Chinese notions of *fengshui* or geomancy. Stretching skywards, and casting unwelcome shadows over auspicious sites and shrines, steeples in particular were seen as having a disturbing effect on the harmony of the elements. As a result, countless local misfortunes, whether they be drought or illness, were attributed to the ill effects of the buildings which missionaries constructed.

The growth of anti-foreign feeling was not simply a product of missionary activity. Among the educated élite there was widespread resentment against the foreigner's privileged position in China. Extraterritoriality—the right of a foreigner not to be tried by a Chinese court—special customs privileges, and anti-Chinese exclusionary rules for foreign-run schools, recreational facilities, and residential areas fed the flames of anti-foreign feeling.

The Empress Dowager or 'Old Buddha'. At first she tried to stamp out the Boxers, seeing them as a threat to the dynasty. Later, however, she secretly supported their aims to drive the foreigners from China.

Two other developments coincided with the rise of anti-foreign sentiment in late nineteenth-century China. The first was the consolidation of power at the Chinese Imperial Court of a group of ultra-conservative officials led by the Empress Dowager Cixi. Bitterly opposed to a short-lived program of reform instituted by her young nephew, the Emperor Guangxu, in 1898 the Empress Dowager pushed the Emperor aside and resumed her earlier position as all-powerful Regent. From this post she and her supporters resisted all proposals for change to the now ineffectual and corrupt Manchu State structure.

In the years immediately preceding the Boxer Troubles, the Emperor Guangxu attempted to introduce changes to the moribund imperial system. His 'One Hundred Days of Reform' were vigorously opposed by the Empress Dowager and the conservative faction at court. In 1898 he was shunted aside, the Empress Dowager assumed the Regency and once again became the real power behind the Dragon Throne.

The second development was the growing precariousness of China's economic condition, especially in the rural areas. During the late 1890s a series of natural calamities struck northern China. Unseasonably hot weather led to drought for two years in a row. In subsequent years, locusts destroyed crops in hundreds of villages. Then came a period of floods. After each disaster harvests failed and famine followed. Desperation in the villages coupled with deepening anti-foreign sentiment and the return to power of the corrupt and backward-looking conservatives in Peking proved to be a potent mixture. The result was the outbreak of what has come to be known as the 'Boxer Troubles'.

The *Yihequan* or 'Society of Righteous and Harmonious Fists'—disdainfully dubbed 'Boxers' by the foreign community —first emerged as a secret society among rural peasants in Shandong Province in the mid-1890s. By the end of the decade the ranks of their fanatical members had swollen to such an extent that they shook China's last imperial dynasty to its very foundation.

The aims of the Boxers were simple—death to foreigners, and an end to foreign influence in China. The message was spread by a co-ordinated and novel propaganda drive throughout the towns and villages of North China. In the market-places huge red banners were strung bearing such inscriptions as 'Assist China to exterminate the foreigners!' and 'Death and destruction to the foreigner and all his works!' In addition, Boxer supporters distributed small handbills vividly portraying in bright hand-painted colours the insults to which China had been subjected at the hands of the foreigners and the negative effects of Western influence. These primitive cartoons were often accompanied by a printed text which blamed China's economic and political woes on the spread of Western religion and technology. A card distributed in Peking in 1899 stated: 'Disturbances are to be dreaded from the foreign devils; everywhere they are starting missions, erecting telegraphs, and building railways.' *The Shanghai Mercury* in the same year reprinted a box of placards which included the following inscription: 'On account of the Protestant and Catholic religions the Buddhist gods are oppressed, and our Sages thrust into the background. The anger of heaven and earth has been aroused and a timely rain has consequently been withheld from us.'

Chinese Christian converts and churches were the initial targets of the Boxers. Only later did they turn their attention to the foreigners inside the Legations. ▼ ▶

The costume and demeanor of the Boxers were as dramatic and inflammatory as their propaganda. Dressed in peasant clothing girded with red and yellow sashes and wearing a bright turban frequently stained with the blood of its owner, the Boxer warrior armed himself with a combination of rusted flintlocks, spears, tridents, and two-handed swords and approached his victims with the high-pitched cry of '*Sha! Sha!*' ('Kill, kill!'). In the late Victorian imagination, the Boxer must have seemed the very incarnation of the Devil himself.

A photograph of a 'real live Boxer' in 1900. The Boxer warriors dressed in brightly coloured clothing and wore headbands and religious amulets to protect them from foreign bullets. Their battle cry was, 'SHA! SHA!' ('Kill! Kill!').

For the Chinese peasant—from whom most Boxer warriors were drawn—the appeal of the Boxers lay not simply in their message and their costume. Rather, as the Reverend Arthur Smith has observed, it was 'the supernatural element in the Boxer claims which gave the savage the powerful hold upon the popular imagination and the popular faith.' Most important of these claims was the indestructibility of the Boxer himself. Because of the righteousness of their cause, Boxers believed that they were invulnerable to rifle or cannon fire. According to one contemporary observer, A.H. Savage-Landor, Buddhist monks preached that: 'Rifle or cannon bullets or pieces of shell may strike a Boxer in any part of his anatomy, but cannot penetrate the body of a sacred member. When hit, the bullet will bounce back without injuring him in the slightest degree.'

Demonstrations of the Boxers' spiritual powers were a common feature of village meetings and Boxer rallies in the late 1890s. Like magicians at a village theatre, Boxer recruiters revealed their powers in well-rehearsed shows. Accompanied by incantations and trances, such demonstrations served to underscore the Boxers' special relationship with powerful spiritual forces.

The first targets of the Boxers' wrath were the Chinese Christian converts—'secondary devils' or *er maozi* as they were called. In the early phase, the Boxers restricted their campaigns to harassment of Chinese Christians. Gradually, however, the violence escalated. Soon, the homes of converts were burned, their churches desecrated. Later the converts themselves were subjected to torture and in many cases death. The violence against Chinese Christians fed the Boxers' confidence. Soon their attacks spread to the foreign devils themselves.

The first foreign victim of Boxer violence was a young English missionary named S.M. Brooks who was murdered in late December 1899. The circumstances of his death were reported in the *North China Herald*:

[The Boxers] saw Mr. Brooks coming on his way, and, hastily putting on red head-cloths, they rushed out and attacked him; in the attack he was wounded. They then stripped him to his underclothing and left him tied up outside in the bitter cold. At night they took him to Maokiapu, which he reached much exhausted from exposure and his wounds. There he broke away, but was soon overtaken, and his head was cut off.

Although the Reverend Brooks' murderer was later arrested by the Chinese and executed in the presence of a British Legation official, Boxer attacks against foreigners increased. In the year following the young missionary's death, more than 200 foreign men, women, and children living and working in Chinese communities outside Peking were killed. The cruelty of the Boxers was widely publicized in China, mainly through the English-language press. One of the most widely reported incidents was the 'martyrdom' of a group of Christian missionaries in Taiyuanfu in 1900. The report of a Chinese eyewitness to the massacre was carried in full in the *North China Herald*:

The first to be led forth was Pastor Farthing. His wife clung to him, but he gently put her aside and going in front of the soldiers, himself knelt down without saying a word, and his head was struck off by one blow of the executioner's knife.

He was quickly followed by Pastors Hoddle and Beynon, Drs. Lovitt and Wilson, all of whom were beheaded with one blow . . . . When the men were finished, the ladies were taken. Mrs. Farthing had hold of the hands of her children who clung to her, but the soldiers parted them, and with one blow beheaded their mother. The executioner beheaded all the children and did it skilfully, needing only one blow; but the soldiers were clumsy, and some of the ladies suffered several cuts before death. Mrs. Lovitt was wearing her spectacles and held the hand of her little boy even when she was killed . . . A soldier took off the spectacles before beheading her, which needed two blows.

By May 1900 it was clear to the foreign community in the Peking Legations that the Boxer menace was moving ever closer. On 17 May news reached the French Legation that more than 60 Chinese converts had been murdered in a Boxer attack on a village only 90 miles from the capital. On the next day, 18 May, the British Legation received word from the London Mission Society of a Boxer assault on a mission station only 40 miles from Peking. Rumours of new Boxer atrocities swirled about the Legation Quarter nearly every day.

One of the first in the Legation community to perceive the Boxers' true intentions was the Monsignor Favier, the Vicar-Apostolic of Peking. A long-time resident of the capital, with close connections to Manchu officials, the Monsignor wrote to the French Minister warning of the danger to the Legations and urging the Diplomatic Corps to take precautionary measures. The Monsignor wrote:

This religious persecution is only a facade; the ultimate aim is the extermination of all Europeans. . . . The Boxers' accomplices await them in Peking; they mean to attack the churches first, then the Legations. For us in our Cathedral, the date of the attack has actually been fixed. Everybody knows it, it is the talk of the town.

Impressed by Favier's views, the French Minister raised the matter with the diplomatic corps in a meeting held on 20 May. However, nothing was done. Eight days later, a large Boxer force attacked the railway station at Fengtai, the main connection point on the line between Beijing and Tianjin. The attack left a number of foreign engineers and their families stranded. A group of Legation residents decided to take matters into their own hands. Armed with revolvers, the group left the Legation Quarter on horseback led by Auguste Chamot, the owner of the Hôtel de Pékin, and his young wife. They returned later in the evening having rescued 29 Europeans.

The events at Fengtai at last spurred the diplomatic corps into action. A message was sent to Tianjin and preparations were made for the despatch of additional guards to the Legations. A train containing 337 men from the American, British, French, Italian, Japanese, and Russian forces in Tianjin set out in the early morning of 31 May 1900. Three days later the Germans sent an additional force of 52 soldiers and the Austrians despatched 37 men. The arrival of reinforcements for the Legation Guards bolstered, at least temporarily, the courage of the foreigners in Peking. However, the euphoria quickly vanished. Attacks against foreign missionaries still in the countryside outside Peking were intensified. Furthermore, the Boxers directed their energy to the dismantling of the railway line over which the reinforcements had arrived from Tianjin. By 4 June, the stations along the railway line were in flames.

Concerned about the growing violence and the proximity to Peking of the recent Boxer attacks, the Legations filed formal protests with the Zongli Yamen. However, it soon became clear that the Chinese Government, which had previously branded the Boxers 'bandits', had now thrown its weight behind them. In an Edict issued on 6 June, the Empress Dowager expressed sympathy for the Boxer cause and placed the blame for the current unrest on the missionaries and other foreigners. As news of the Imperial Edict spread, foreign missionaries abandoned their stations and streamed into central Peking, seeking refuge inside the Legations. The diplomatic corps met again on 9 June. At the close of this meeting the British Minister, Sir Claude MacDonald, was instructed to call for further reinforcements from Tianjin.

Sir Claude MacDonald, British Minister in Peking during the Siege. An influential member of the diplomatic corps, Sir Claude was later given command of the Legation Volunteers and was put in overall charge of the defence of the Legations.

On the next day, a special train carrying 2,129 officers and troops under the command of Admiral Sir Edward Seymour departed from Tianjin. The force comprised soldiers of each of the eight Powers, the British supplying the largest number (915), and the Austrians the smallest (6). The troops carried with them seven large field guns, ten machine guns, hundreds of pistols and rifles and thousands of pounds of ordnance.

On 14 June, Admiral Seymour, then *en route*, sent a handwritten note by 'runner' to Sir Claude to inform him that help was on the way. He also remarked that his progress was being hindered due to Boxer attacks. But he stated that these had been repulsed and that the Boxers had been 'killed in large numbers.' The letter ended on an optimistic note: 'All will yet be well!' Unfortunately, Seymour was wrong. Neither he nor his forces ever reached Peking. Attacked by Boxer troops and regular units of the Chinese Imperial Army, Seymour's train was halted at An Ping, slightly more than half way to Peking.

As the foreign community in the Legation Quarter saw the Boxers approaching, they sent for reinforcements from Tianjin. On 10 June 1900, more than 2,000 officers and men left for Peking under the command of Admiral Sir Edward Seymour. En route, Sir Edward sent a handwritten message by runner to Sir Claude in Peking. Dated 14 June, the message informed Sir Claude that the troop train's arrival in Peking would be delayed due to persistent attacks by Boxers. He ended, however, on an optimistic note: 'All will yet be well!' In the event, Seymour and his decimated troops never reached Peking.

53

When news of Seymour's predicament reached Tianjin, the Powers demanded that the Chinese troops evacuate the Dagu forts which guarded the entrance into Tianjin from the sea. The Chinese Government, however, chose to ignore the demand and instead ordered its troops to open fire on the European ships anchored opposite the forts. At the same time, an Imperial Edict was issued declaring war against the foreign Powers. In the end, the foreign navies quickly repulsed the Chinese attacks. The operation cost 172 lives, but it opened the way for the landing of further relief forces from the ships offshore up to Tianjin. These forces proceeded westward to rescue Seymour and his troops and escort them back to Tianjin. All in all, his attempt to reach Peking had proved to be a disaster, leaving 62 dead and 230 wounded.

News of Seymour's retreat did not reach the Peking Legations until several weeks later. The Admiral and his troops had been expected to arrive on 11 June. When the trains did not arrive at Peking Station in the morning, suspicions were aroused. At noon, the greeting party went back to the Legations for lunch to be followed by a report to the diplomatic corps. The Minister of the Japanese Legation, Mr Sugiyama, decided to return to the railway station immediately after lunch. It proved to be a mistake. While on his way to the station, he was attacked by Imperial Troops and his body was cut into pieces before a group of onlookers. Before abandoning his remains, the Chinese troops cut out his heart and had it sent to their Commander.

The failure of Seymour's expedition, coupled with the horrible murder of the Japanese Minister, brought panic to the foreign community. The tension grew even greater two days later when a Boxer was sighted in a cart travelling up the middle of Legation Street itself, brazenly sharpening a long knife. While most foreign residents who witnessed the sight gazed in horror or ran to safety, the German Minister, Baron von Ketteler, sprang into action. Well known for his ill temper, he chased after the Boxer and beat him over the head with his walking stick.

By now, the Boxers had spread throughout the city terrorizing Chinese neighbourhoods in search of missionaries and Chinese converts. Writing about his visit through Peking neighbourhoods outside the Legation Quarter, Dr G.E. Morrison, local correspondent for *The Times* of London, reported seeing 'women and children hacked to pieces, men trussed like fowls, with noses and ears cut off and eyes gouged out'.

Suddenly, on 19 June, the Chinese government presented the foreigners inside the Legation with an ultimatum. Set out in elegant calligraphy, enclosed in large red envelopes, the message from the Chinese stated as follows:

The Boxer movement is now active in the capital and there is much popular excitement. While your excellency and the members of your family . . . reside here the Legations are in danger, and the Chinese government is really in a difficult position as regards affording efficient protection. The Yamen must, therefore, request that within 24 hours your excellency will start, accompanied by the Legation guards, who must be kept under proper control, and proceed to Tianjin in order to prevent any unforeseen calamity.

The diplomatic corps convened immediately to consider an appropriate response. Eventually, it was agreed that the Legations had no alternative but to comply with the Chinese request. Accordingly, a formal reply was drafted including a special request that further time be granted to the foreigners so as to better prepare for the evacuation. To discuss the details of their departure, the Ministers also requested a meeting with officials of the Zongli Yamen at 9 a.m. on the following day.

The next morning, 20 June, the diplomatic corps met at the French Legation. As the hour approached nine o'clock, the Ministers still had received no word that the Chinese would agree to meet them. The German Minister, Baron von Ketteler, immediately suspected a snub. Enraged, he insisted on making the short journey to the Yamen himself—with or without an invitation.

Smoking a cigar, and accompanied by his Chinese-speaking secretary, Heinrich Cordes, and an unarmed ceremonial escort, the Baron set off in a sedan chair. On his approach to the Yamen, however, the two Germans were attacked at the northern end of Hatamen Street. Only Cordes lived to tell what happened:

We were close to the police station on the left. I was watching the cart with some lance-bearers passing before the Minister's chair, when suddenly I saw a sight that made my heart stand still. The Minister's chair was three paces in front of me. I saw a banner soldier, apparently a Manchu, in full uniform with a Mandarin's hat and

The murder on 20 June 1900 of Baron von Ketteler, the Chief Minister of the German Legation, electrified the foreign community in Peking. The Baron had been on his way to the Zongli Yamen to discuss the terms of the foreigners' safe passage out of Peking when his sedan chair was attacked by Boxers and imperial troops. Arrogant and ill-tempered, von Ketteler was disliked by the Chinese. His death had been reported in the London newspapers on 16 June— four days before it actually occurred. The mystery has never been fully explained.

a button and blue feather, step forward, present his rifle within a yard of the chair window, levelled *[sic]* it at the Minister's head and fired. I shouted in terror, 'Halt!' At the same moment the shot rang out, the chairs were thrown down. I sprang to my feet. A shot struck me in the lower part of the body. Others were fired at me. I saw the Minister's chair standing, but there was no movement.

Herr Cordes, severely wounded, fled down the street into the safety of the American Methodist Mission hospital. The Baron's body was dragged by the Chinese to the Zongli Yamen.

News of von Ketteler's death was met with little surprise in Europe: it had been reported in the London papers on 16 June, four days before it actually occurred! A simple coincidence? Or had the attack on von Ketteler been planned by the Chinese in advance? No explanation has ever been found.

56

Some weeks later, the Chinese soldier who shot and killed von Ketteler, a Manchu named Enhai, was found and arrested by Japanese troops. After a trial conducted by the Germans, he was taken to the spot where the murder was committed and was decapitated. Before his execution, he said: 'I received orders from my sergeant to kill every foreigner that came up the street; I am a soldier and I only know it is my duty to obey orders.'

A Manchu soldier named Enhai was later arrested for Baron von Ketteler's murder. Shown here, manacled, Enhai was put on trial by the Germans, convicted and then brought to the site of the Baron's murder, where he was decapitated.

The murder of Baron von Ketteler occurred less than five hours before the expiry of the evacuation order given on the previous day by the Chinese. Originally accepted by the foreigners, many now believed that the evacuation would be tantamount to suicide. Accordingly, the Legations decided to brace themselves for their defence. Women and children, missionaries, and other non-combatants were sent into the British Legation, the largest and best defended of the foreign compounds in the Quarter. The total number of foreigners now resident within the compound was in excess of 900.

57

Outside the British Legation compound were nearly 2,000 Chinese Christians who were soon set to work building barricades against the impending attack. The Legation Guards and civilian volunteers took up defence positions along the perimeter. The regular guard strength, including reinforcements sent earlier from Peking, totalled slightly over 400 men. In addition, a little over 125 civilians volunteered to join in the fight.

Chinese Christians flooded the British Legation from all over Peking on news that the Boxers would soon attack the city. This photograph shows three Chinese converts inside the main courtyard of the Legation.

The Chinese ultimatum expired at 4 p.m. on the afternoon of 20 June. Soon thereafter the Boxers began their attack. The ferocity and strength of the Boxers surprised the foreign defenders. In short order the Belgian and Dutch Legations located outside the centre of the Quarter were quickly abandoned. Later, the Austrian Legation Guards were forced back from the barricades to seek refuge behind the walls of the French Legation. The outer defences collapsed completely on 22 June. Surprised by a sudden barrage of fire, the Legation Guards abandoned their posts at the eastern end of the defences, leaving more than two thirds of the Legation Quarter in the hands of the Boxers.

The British Legation now became the central refuge and focus of defence for the foreign community. To facilitate co-ordination of the defence, it was decided that the guards of the various Legations, together with the volunteers, would be put under the command of Sir Claude MacDonald, the British Minister.

The British Legation became the central refuge for the foreign community during the Siege. It was also the focus of Boxer attacks after the Legation volunteers were forced to abandon the outer lines of defence and retreat within its gates. As this photograph shows, the main gates were barricaded against the attacks. The fighting began soon after 4:00 p.m. on 20 June 1900.

Many of the Chinese Christians were put to work building barricades on the perimeters of the British Legation.

The Boxers and the Imperial Troops soon redeployed to take advantage of the concentration of foreigners inside the British Legation. On 23 June, Chinese troops took up positions on the top of buildings near the Mongol Market and fired down inside the British Legation. Others set fire to the buildings surrounding the Legation. As the foreigners inside fought with their water buckets to keep the fire from spreading, the wind suddenly shifted. As a result the British Legation was spared. Unfortunately, however, the flames ravaged the ancient timber buildings of the Hanlin Academy next door. Thousands of priceless books, many centuries old, were destroyed in the fire, depriving China of one of her greatest cultural treasures.

Suddenly, without explanation, the firing stopped. Chinese officials sent word to the Legations that a despatch was to be delivered to the foreigners from the Imperial Palace. Within the Legations, there was widespread hope that the Siege would be lifted. However, the promised despatch never arrived, and three hours later the fighting resumed.

The First Secretary's house inside the British Legation, sandbagged against Boxer attacks.

▼

The situation now became more serious than ever. News reached the Legations that a new Imperial Edict, issued on 24 June, called for the extermination of the foreigners. The edict contained an Imperial charge to all Chinese, which read: 'Whenever you meet a foreigner, you must kill him; whenever he retreats, you must kill him at once.' Since telegraph communications to Tianjin were now cut off, frantic efforts were made to send handwritten messages to the coast by Chinese 'runners'. One such message, despatched on 24 June, was written in the hand of Sir Robert Hart, the Inspector General of the Imperial Maritime Customs. Its simple message was: 'Beseiged in British Legation. Situation desperate. Make haste!'

As the attacks continued through July, conditions inside the British Legation worsened. The belltower served as a kind of message centre and gathering place for foreign ladies, soldiers, and Chinese Christians.

As the Boxers intensified their attacks, living conditions inside the British Legation became increasingly difficult. The foreign community sustained itself largely on rations of pony meat from the Legation's polo stables, mixed with rice. Sanitary conditions deteriorated as a result of the overcrowding. The nauseating stench from the dead bodies lying in the Peking summer heat outside the Legation walls was said to be overwhelming. Sickness was widespread, and at least six children died. The makeshift hospital set up inside the Legation residence was poorly equipped and most of the patients were forced to lie on the floor.

The Siege also imposed an enormous emotional strain on the foreign community. It proved too much for some. At least one foreigner, a Norwegian, is reported to have gone mad. At one point, he left the Legation, went out into the Chinese lines, and proceeded to inform the Chinese troops of ways by which they might improve the accuracy of their fire. He was subsequently allowed by the Chinese to leave unharmed, and he returned to the Legation. He was promptly seized and locked into a shed for the duration of the hostilities.

As the weeks dragged on, the fighting continued unabated. An event which caused a temporary rise in the spirits of the foreign defenders was the discovery in early July of an old cannon. The armament was refurbished and repaired and quickly put to use against the Boxers. Dubbed the 'International', but more commonly referred to as 'Old Betsy', its heavy charges were fired in the direction of the Boxer Command, taking the Chinese completely by surprise.

In July, the foreign defenders found an old cannon which they refurbished and put to use against the Boxers. It successfully repelled a number of attacks and caused surprise among the Chinese troops. Christened the 'International' but often referred to as 'Old Betsy', the gun was manned by British and American Legation guards.

On 15 July, the Siege took yet another strange turn. A message was smuggled into the British compound from the Zongli Yamen. Addressed to Sir Claude MacDonald, the message stated only that the Chinese Government would do its utmost to protect the foreigners inside the Legations. Five days later, another note arrived from the Yamen. This message stated that an Imperial Decree had been issued on the preceding day ordering that, in view of Peking's unusually hot weather, fruit and vegetables were to be sent to the Legations.

▲

'Old Betsy's' makeshift firing platform inside the British Legation.

There followed several days of truce. On 25 July yet another message was received. This message reiterated the earlier Chinese request that the foreigners abandon the Legations and leave Peking immediately. The request was never complied with. By the beginning of August the fighting had resumed. In the meantime, a frenzy of diplomatic activity was taking place in the capitals of Europe. By 3 August, arrangements had been put in place for the despatch of an International Relief Force to Peking. Commanders of the foreign forces anchored off the coast were duly notified and the international force left Tianjin within the week. Consisting of nearly 20,000 men, almost half of whom were Japanese, the force proceeded along the Beihe River and arrived at Tongzhou on

12 August. There the soldiers rested while their leaders devised a plan for the final assault on Peking.

The plan called for near simultaneous assaults by different units against strategic points in Peking. Despite its brilliance, the plan's execution collapsed due to a lack of co-ordination. Different forces arrived in the wrong places at the wrong times and some got lost entirely.

Eventually, at about 3 p.m. on the afternoon of 13 August, British forces were sighted approaching the Tartar City Wall at the southern perimeter of the Legation Quarter. A signaller sent out the following message: 'Come in by sewer'. British soldiers—Sikhs sent from India—quickly removed the grill from the bottom of the Water Gate underneath the wall and entered the Legation Quarter up Canal Road. The Americans and others soon followed.

The International Relief Forces arrived in Peking from Tianjin in the late afternoon of 13 August 1900. The first to enter the Legation Quarter were Sikh troops from British India.

As the Relief forces swarmed into the Legation Quarter, the Boxers and Imperial troops were soon dislodged from their positions and fled. The exhausted members of the foreign community shut up inside the British Legation realized that the trials of the last 55 days were now over. With tears of joy streaming down their faces, the foreigners ran to welcome their rescuers. One British resident described the scene as follows:

Sir Claude MacDonald took special pride in the fact that troops under British command were the first to enter the Legations and break the Siege. In a letter to the Foreign Office he wrote: 'It was a tremendous score our people being in first'. He later posed with a gathering of British marines. But where were the Sikhs?

▼

◄

The Sikh soldiers made their entrance into the city through the Water Gate which penetrated the Tartar Wall at the southern end of British Road.

Men, women and children, every one out on the lawn, cheering, yelling, crying, mad with excitement and delight; and there coming in, line after line, waving their turbans and cheering, real, live, big, burly Indian troops, dripping with perspiration, covered with dust, and thoroughly tired. I rushed up to the first one I saw; I clapped him on the back; I shook his hand; I yelled, I cheered. My pent-up feelings had to be relieved in some way. I, who had thought I should never come out of this awful siege alive, could now realize and see that I was at last saved!

▲

The Relief ended 55 days of suffering for the foreign community trapped in the Legations. The end of the ordeal was greeted with wild dancing and celebrations in the streets of the Quarter.

Although the Legations were now secure, the Siege was not over for all of Peking's foreign community. A smaller group of less than 100 foreigners, and more than 3,000 Chinese converts inside the Northern Cathedral, or Beitang, several miles outside the Quarter, were still under attack. Trapped throughout the Siege inside the Cathedral grounds, this group had in fact suffered far more than any of the ministers and their families who weathered the storm of the previous weeks inside the British Legation. Defended by only 43 French and Italian sailors with limited arms and ammunition, the Catholic missionaries led by Monsignor Favier, together with the Chinese converts, suffered unspeakable hardships. For them, the Relief forces had come none too soon. On the night of 12 August, as foreigners in the Legations celebrated their imminent rescue, the Boxers detonated a bomb underneath the building alongside the Cathedral where 22 Sisters of Charity had gathered the children for protection. More than 100 people were killed in the blast, most of whom were infants and children. Half-starved and having nearly given up all hope of rescue, the Cathedral's remaining inhabitants were saved on the morning of 16 August with the arrival of a mixed rescue party of Japanese, French, Russian and British troops.

The summer of 1900 left 76 foreigners dead and 179 wounded inside the Legation Quarter alone. Several thousand foreign missionaries died at the hands of the Boxers throughout the provinces. The number of Chinese casualties is unknown.

The British Legation cemetery. The Siege left 76 foreigners dead. There is no record of how many Boxers and imperial troops died during the fighting.

▼

V

The Aftermath

◄

The Siege left a large part of the Legation Quarter and its environs devastated. The destruction extended as far as the Qianmen, shown here, which was badly damaged by fire.

THE RELIEF OF the Legations did little to restore the peace in Peking. In fact, just the opposite occurred. Bent on retribution and spurred on by a lust for booty, the Allied Expeditionary Forces remained in the capital for more than a year.

One person who saw early on that the arrival of foreign troops in Peking would be unlikely to restore the *status quo ante* was the Empress Dowager. Advised by her inner circle late in the evening on 14 August that she would likely be killed if caught by the Relief forces, 'Old Buddha', as she was affectionately called by her loyal eunuchs in the palace, decided to flee. At 4 a.m. on the following morning, the Empress and her entire court retinue disguised themselves as Chinese peasants and secretly departed from the capital. After a journey of more than 700 miles which lasted nearly two months, the court re-established itself in the north-western city of Xian. The flight was announced as an 'autumn inspection tour'. The Empress Dowager left a city which had been nearly brought to its knees even before the arrival of the Relief forces. As a result of the chaos brought about by the Boxers' occupation of Peking and the fighting over the summer, many ordinary Chinese residents of the city had been killed and even larger numbers had fled in fear of their lives. As a result, by the time of the Relief the city's population had been reduced to about one-quarter of its normal size.

News of the arrival of the Relief forces was greeted with terror by Peking residents, especially Manchu officials and their families. Many tried to flee. In the panic which ensued, a number of Manchu nobles had only time enough to save themselves and a few prized possessions. Left behind were their numerous wives and concubines, many of whom chose death at their own hands over the uncertainties which faced them in an occupied capital.

One foreign resident of Peking, the Reverend Arthur Smith, described the scene in the aftermath of the Siege in the following terms:

From the Russian and the American Legations west to the Ch'ien Mên for a width of many hundred yards and over a quarter of a mile in length there is now a stretch without a single building intact. A similar devastation is seen to the north of the northern gate of the Imperial City, and on a smaller scale in multitudes of other places as well. When it was possible for foreigners again to traverse the streets of Peking, the desolation which met the eye was appalling. Dead bodies of soldiers lay in heaps, or singly, in some instances covered with a torn old mat, but always a prey to the now well-fed dogs. Dead dogs and horses poisoned the air of every region. Huge pools of stagnant water were reeking with rotting corpses of man and beast . . . For miles upon miles of the busiest streets of the Northern and Southern Cities not a single shop was open for business, and scarcely a dozen persons were anywhere to be seen.

Walking down Legation Street after the Siege, one could go for nearly a quarter of a mile and see nothing but the burnt out shells of former Legation buildings.

In the months following the lifting of the Siege, the numbers of allied troops stationed in China increased as a result of the arrival of reinforcements from abroad. By Autumn 1900 the official figures for the foreign forces were: 8,000 Japanese, 5,000 Russians, 3,000 British, 2,000 Americans, 2,000 Germans, 1,500 French and several hundred Italians and Austrians.

The allies decided that the troops could best be deployed by dividing the city into occupation zones. Each of the national forces was assigned responsibility for a zone. Its troops were charged with the two-fold task of weeding out the remnants of Boxer fighters in the area and restoring and maintaining public order there. As it turned out, the former was accomplished quite quickly, at least within the confines of the Peking City walls. The latter, however, was only achieved after a much longer period of time.

In their search for hostile Boxer forces, the foreign troops in each zone divided themselves into smaller bands which patrolled the various *hutong*, often going from house to house.

Unable to distinguish between genuine Boxers—who by now had shed their colourful garb—and ordinary Chinese citizens, anyone who appeared hostile to the foreign troops was liable to be seized. Many Chinese who were taken into custody were very quickly sentenced, usually without trial, to execution. The execution was in most cases carried out in the Chinese manner, decapitation, by Chinese professionals and in public. The 'Boxer trials' soon became popular events for residents of the Legation Quarter in the days following the Siege, and foreigners were frequent spectators at the executions.

'Boxer Trials'—the summary arrest and execution of suspected Boxers—were a common occurrence in the days immediately after the Siege. Public decapitation was usually the final stage of the proceedings. The events attracted crowds of spectators, including both Chinese and foreigners.

72

Not surprisingly, many Peking residents who had not fled the city remained in their houses 'cowed', as one contemporary observer noted, 'like whipped hounds in their kennels'. In an attempt to discourage attacks by the foreign troops, many Chinese residents painted foreign flags on their doors or flew hand-made foreign banners from makeshift poles erected on their courtyard walls.

This house inside the British Legation compound was hit repeatedly by Chinese cannon.

Both Chinese and foreign accounts of the occupation of Peking indicate that the Germans were by far the most aggressive of the foreigners. The messianic fervour with which the Germans approached the task of 'punishing' the Chinese is best illustrated by the words of the German Emperor in a speech delivered to German troops departing for China on 27 July. He said:

When you meet a foe you will defeat him. No quarter will be given, no prisoners will be taken. Let all who fall into your hands be at your mercy. Just as the Huns a thousand years ago, under the leadership of Etzel, gained a reputation by virtue of which they still live in historical tradition, so may the name of Germany become known in such a manner in China, that no Chinese will ever again even dare to look askance at a German.

The main building of the German Legation after the Siege.

The Russian Legation suffered extensive damage during the Siege. Here, the remains of the Chancery Building are guarded by Russian marines.

The British Legation's buildings, the main target of the Boxers' attack during the final stages of the Siege, were also badly damaged.

The hatred and bitterness which found expression in the Emperor's message was, in part at least, attributable to the genuine shock with which Germans greeted the news of the murder of their beloved Baron von Ketteler. The shock very quickly transformed itself into outrage when on 16 August the Baron's body was found unceremoniously deposited in an old wooden crate inside the Zongli Yamen. Only weeks before, Chinese

75

officials had sent written assurances to the Baroness von Ketteler that her husband's body was 'lying in state' at the Yamen. Seen as further proof of Chinese duplicity, the matter was not soon forgotten. The Baron's remains were reinterred on the following day in the garden of the German Legation.

Baron von Ketteler's body lying in state before the devastated main building of the German Legation. His body had been removed from the Zongli Yamen where it was found after the Siege. After a funeral arranged by the Baron's widow, his remains were reportedly interred in the rear of the German Legation compound.

More than retribution, however, was on the minds of the German politicians and military officers who offered their whole-hearted support to the occupation. The fact is that, because of their late arrival in Peking, the Germans had, for the most part, missed out on the main action during the Relief. As a result, Germany was keen to claim its share of the glory during the occupation period. Germany's intentions to play a leading role in the occupation of Peking were made known to the allies in early August. At that time, each of the allies received a telegram from the Emperor of Russia recommending that the naming of a German to assume the supreme command of the Allied Expeditionary Forces 'would be of advantage'. After some hesitation and backstage manoeuvring, agreement was finally reached among the eight foreign Powers. Soon thereafter, Field Marshall Count von Waldersee, a distinuished German military commander, was named the first Supreme Allied Commander of modern times.

After the arrival of von Waldersee in Peking, the pace of the punitive expeditions launched by the allied armies in and around Peking was stepped up. They continued well into the

The Field Marshall Count von Waldersee, Commander-in-Chief of the Allied Forces in Peking, being seen off at the station in Germany by his wife upon his departure for China. The Count was to later become famous for his punitive expeditions against Boxer remnants in and around Peking during the aftermath of the Siege.

year 1901. Indeed, during the first quarter of that year more than 40 campaigns were conducted by the allies under von Waldersee's command. Many of these expeditions were little more than legally sanctioned looting raids. As they fled the city, wealthy Manchus left behind large quantities of cash, jewellery, precious antiques and other valuables. Their now-empty houses were left unguarded, leaving the treasures within waiting to be claimed by the first passer-by. As the historian H.B. Morse noted, the sacking of Peking was conducted 'riotously, but systematically'. In his summing up of the situation, Morse stated:

The troops were out of hand and looked on Peking and all it contained, persons and property, as prize of war, subject to their will; and . . . as China had broken the law of nations and defied the world, the world in its turn recognized none of its own laws in its treatment of the law-breaker.

77

Among the occupying forces, the Russian troops were almost universally condemned by contemporary witnesses for their 'ferocity and careless cruelty'. The French also fared poorly in written accounts of the post-Siege days. They acquired a reputation for having looted 'methodically and thoroughly' and were accused of 'unspeakable excesses'. The Germans also engaged in looting with apparent enthusiasm. Their rapaciousness reached a high point when the German military authorities determined to remove a number of the instruments contained in the Chinese Imperial Observatory, which lay within the German zone, to Berlin. The Observatory, set up more than two centuries earlier by Jesuit missionaries, was one of China's most unique ancient treasures. In a letter to the German Kaiser, Count von Waldersee admitted that the instruments were Chinese property. However, he nonetheless recommended their confiscation on the grounds that 'in accordance with the custom universally prevailing here [they] were to be regarded as German war booty'. The German plan was later complicated by the French who also asserted claims to several astrological instruments. Eventually a deal was struck by the two Powers to divide the Observatory's contents between them. Soon thereafter, the instruments were shipped to Europe. Some, but not all, were returned to Peking in the years following Germany's defeat in World War I.

Japanese troops are said to have been by far the best behaved of all the foreign forces in Peking. In retrospect, however, it appears that the reasons for this apparently meritorious behaviour had less to do with honesty and discipline than efficiency. Soon after the Japanese command was assigned its occupation zone, Japanese troops proceeded directly to the Imperial Ministry of Revenue where they carted off two to three million taels of silver. The treasure was later deposited inside the Japanese Legation. Japanese troops next turned to the Chinese imperial granaries, silk stores and armories in their occupation zone. By the beginning of October, more than 15,000 tons of rice, 1,400 swords, 67 guns, 2,988 rifles and a large amount of other strategic items had been moved to the Japanese Legation.

As the German and Japanese cases illustrate, looting was not confined to foreign footsoldiers temporarily gone astray. The thirst for booty could even be found among the highest ranks of the military. One Russian general, for example, is reported to have returned home with ten trunks loaded with treasures stolen from

Manchu palaces. Even the wife of the upright British minister Sir Claude MacDonald was reported to have on at least one occasion 'devoted herself most earnestly to looting'.

One of the most graphic accounts of the 'looting fever' which gripped foreigners in Peking in the days following the Siege was provided by Polly Condit Smith, a friend of the wife of the first Secretary of the American Legation, who found herself trapped in Peking during a visit in July 1900. Miss Smith wrote:

Yesterday, I was en route from the British Legation to the American, when a big Sikh addressed me most respectfully, whacking his chest, which was bulging in tremendous curves: 'Mem-sahib give me two dollars, I give memsahib [sic] nice things.' There had just been an order issued to all British troops that the loot they procured each day must be turned in to some appointed official, so I fancied that this man must have wanted to get rid of something which he might find difficult to explain if found on his person. I, of course, had no money with me—it was the one thing we had had no use for for two months—but I returned to our Legation and procured two dollars, for my curiosity was aroused, and returning hastily to where I had left my man standing; and then, in the most evident perturbation, he unloaded what he thought was only a proper equivalent for the two dollars which he had asked of me—an exquisite gold-mounted cloisonné clock and two huge, struggling hens! . . .

This morning Baron von Rahden came for breakfast, our conversation being, as usual, carried on in French. He told me he had procured for me a good sable coat—and when a Russian speaks of good sables they are good, for that nationality are expert judges of furs. I wanted to accept the coat in the spirit it was offered, as a testimonial of a charming friendship, formed under extraordinary circumstances, but owing to the intrinsic value of the garment I had to decline it. I don't think he understood very well my refusing it, and I had within an hour the pleasure of seeing him present it to another woman, who accepted it without a qualm, and without giving him, I thought, very many thanks. My soul was torn with conflicting emotions all day, and in the afternoon a Belgian, of whom I had seen a good deal during the Siege, brought me a tortoise-shell bracelet, set with handsome pearls, which he had taken from the arm of a Chinese officer whom he had killed. I surprised myself by promptly accepting it. My nerves could not have stood it, and I took it rather than have a repetition of the sequel to the sable-coat episode.

The foreign preoccupation with punitive expeditions and looting in the weeks and months following the Relief, deflected the attention of the Diplomatic Corps away from the question of pursuing peace talks with the Chinese. The only decision reached among the Powers at the first meeting of the diplomatic conference on 18 August was to stage a victory parade within the Imperial Palace grounds. With the Russians leading the way, followed by the Japanese, Americans, and Europeans, the troops of the Allied Expeditionary Force filed passed the reviewing stand on which stood the ministers of the eight foreign Powers.

▲
The Allied Forces who occupied Peking after the Siege divided the city up into separate occupation zones. The commander of the forces in each zone was responsible for the maintenance of peace and order. However, looting was widespread. This photograph is a group portrait of the Commanders of the International Forces.

Although one account of the parade describes the whole affair as having been rather boring, it is hard to imagine how this could have been the case. With goose-stepping Germans, Sikhs playing bagpipes, and the short Japanese soldiers in fresh, white dress uniform marching stiffly between the British and Americans, the 'victory parade' of 1901 must have been one of the most fascinating inter-cultural jamborees of the twentieth century. In any event, what happened at the parade was less important in the minds of the organizers than that the parade did happen and that it happened within the Imperial City. As Sir Claude MacDonald noted, the site was chosen intentionally 'lest the Chinese, with their infinite capacity for misrepresentation, should infer that some supernatural power had intervened, so that the allied forces had been affected by fear of the consequences of invading the secret crescents.'

Peace talks aimed at formalizing the terms of China's punishment for the throne's complicity in the Boxer Troubles were commenced in late 1900. The talks progressed slowly, as Western diplomats were outmanoeuvered by officials of the Zongli Yamen.

The parade over, new efforts were made by the foreign Powers to formulate the proposed terms of a peace. Progress on this front, however, was impeded by a number of factors. One was the clear lack of consensus among the Powers as to what demands should be made on the Chinese. Some insisted on the punishment of court officials deemed to be 'instigators' of the Boxer troubles before any talks could commence. Others were insisting on even harsher terms. One proposal, for example, called for the destruction of the Imperial Palace and the razing of its walls before the Powers sat down with the Chinese.

Eventually, the talks did begin on Christmas eve of 1900. The meeting was held inside the Spanish Legation. Although the Chinese government had appointed two plenipotentiaries, Li Hong-zhang and Prince Qing, to the talks, only the latter was able to attend the first meeting. Eleven representatives appeared for the foreign Powers. These were: Germany—A. Mumm von

Schwartzenstein; Austria–Hungary—M. Czikann von Wahlborn; Belgium—M. Joostens; Spain—B.J. Day Cologan; United States— W.W. Rockhill; France—Paul Beau; Great Britain—Sir Ernest Sataw; Italy—Marquis Salvago Raggi; Japan—Jutaro Komura; Netherlands— F.M. Knobel; Russia—M. de Giers.

As her representatives negotiated with the foreign Powers, the Empress Dowager was busy polishing her own tarnished image. To foreclose the possibility that the foreign Powers might attempt to hold her personally responsible for the Boxer troubles, during the fall of 1900 and the first half of 1901 she issued a series of imperial edicts calling for the punishment of many of her court advisers who played a role in the Siege. Clearly, the 'Old Buddha' had shifted sides and was now anxious to resume her court in Peking. In June 1901, the Empress Dowager announced her intention to return with her retinue to the capital. After the journey from Xian, she eventually entered Peking through the Qianmen which had been severely damaged by fire in the early days of the Siege. As was the usual custom, she entered by a special gate where she stopped and worshipped before a small shrine. Unknown to her at the time, her passage through the gate had been witnessed by a group of residents of the Legation Quarter who were standing on the ramp above. On seeing the foreigners above her the Empress' reaction took the foreigners by surprise. Whereas just one year earlier she had committed herself to the destruction of the Legation Quarter and the death of its residents, she now offered what appeared to be a sign of friendship. As one observer on the wall that day recorded later:

Before entering the temple where the priests were all ready to begin the ceremony, she stopped once more and, looking up at us, lifted her closed hands under her chin and made a series of little bows.... Something told us that the return of the Court to Peking was a turning-point in history....

That little bow, and the graceful gesture of the closed hands, took us by surprise. From all along the wall there came, in answer, a spontaneous burst of applause. The Empress Dowager appeared pleased. She remained there a few minutes longer, looking up and smiling.

How long the smile lasted, whether it was genuine or feigned, cannot be known. What is clear, however, is that the Peking which the Empress Dowager had returned to was not the same city that she had left. As the ink dried on the peace treaty signed between China and the Western Powers, the once haughty and xenophobic 'Old Buddha' entered a world which had been turned on its head.

The Empress Dowager, who had fled Peking disguised as a peasant in August 1900, returned to the capital the following year. On her entrance into the city she offered a friendly gesture to the foreigners who gathered to witness her return.

VI

The Protocol of 1901

The Final Protocol was signed on 7 September 1901 in Chinese and French. The foreign Powers exacted a heavy price for the Boxer Troubles. Various sanctions were imposed on China and she was made to pay a heavy indemnity. In addition, Article VII of the Protocol gave foreigners exclusive control over the Legation Quarter and granted them the right to 'make it defensible'.

ON 7 SEPTEMBER 1901, several weeks before the Empress Dowager returned to Peking, the Boxer Protocol was signed by the respective representatives of China and the foreign Powers. Consisting of 12 Articles and 19 Annexes, the Protocol set out the terms for the establishment of the post-Siege relationship betweeen China and the allied Powers. Summing up his analysis of the Protocol, the historian H.B. Morse noted: 'For a brief outburst of mid-summer madness . . . China had been required to pay a heavy price.'

A number of the provisions set out in the Protocol required the Manchu Government to take specific action to atone for the atrocities committed by the Boxers. For example, the Germans had insisted on the inclusion of a clause which required that Peking express formal regret for the murder of Baron von Ketteler. This was done in two ways. First, a prince of the Manchu ruling house, representing the Chinese Government, was dispatched to Europe to convey in person to the German Emperor an apology for the Baron's death. Secondly, a monument was erected by China at the site of von Ketteler's murder in Peking. The monument, in the form of a memorial arch or *pai lou*, bore an inscription in Latin, German, and Chinese. It read: 'This Monument is erected in order to point out that what is good, is good; and what is evil, is evil. Let all our subjects learn from the past occurrences and never forget them. We order this.'

The Germans insisted on a clause in the Protocol which obliged the Chinese Government to build a pai-lou, *or memorial arch, at the spot where Baron von Ketteler was killed. The arch contained what foreigners interpreted to be an official apology inscribed in Chinese, German, and Latin. The monument was removed by the Chinese after Germany's defeat in World War I and re-erected in Peking's Central Park.*

PEKING.   Ketteler Monument.

The Chinese also undertook to build a monument in each of the numerous foreign cemeteries which had been desecrated by the Boxers. These included seven cemeteries in Peking (one Russian, one British, and five French) and a number of others on the outskirts of the city. The Chinese were also obliged to raise funds for the erection of monuments within certain foreign cemeteries in the provinces.

▶

China's representative to the peace talks was Li Hong-zhang, an eminent Chinese official and master negotiator.

An early demand pressed by the foreigners during the negotiation of the Protocol was the punishment of imperial officials who were thought to have masterminded the Siege. Accordingly, imperial decrees were issued for the trial and punishment of a large number of high-ranking Manchu officials. As a result, more than a dozen imperial family members and advisers in Peking were sentenced to exile, confiscation of property and death by decapitation. Several others were ordered by imperial decree to commit suicide.

87

The imposition of criminal sanctions on high court officials struck a blow at the very heart of the Manchu State. Yet, the foreign Powers were well aware that the xenophobia which gave birth to the Boxers, and ultimately the Siege itself, was not simply the creation of a handful of court officials. Rather, it was a movement which had also gained support from the Chinese literati or mandarin class, who in most cases were active and virulent opponents of foreign influence in China. In imperial China, the mandarins achieved their position through official examinations administered by Peking. The various degrees granted at various levels of the examination system constituted the 'ladder of success' in traditional Chinese society. Partly as punishment, and partly one suspects, to drive home the point that the fulcrum of power in China had now shifted in favour of the foreigners, the Protocol required the issuance of an imperial decree ordering the suspension of all official examinations for five years in those Chinese cities where 'foreigners were massacred or submitted to cruel treatment'. In all, the ban was ultimately imposed in 45 cities throughout the country.

Another important feature of the Protocol were the provisions relating to the indemnities to be paid by the Chinese Government to the foreign Powers for the damage to person and property which the Powers and their nationals had suffered during the Siege. The entire issue of how the question of the indemnity should be handled was one which generated much controversy among the Powers. During the early stages of the negotiations, several countries, led by the United States, had advanced the view that all claims should be submitted to the arbitral court at the Hague for settlement. Furthermore, America, joined by the Japanese, argued that the final amount of any indemnity should be fixed so as to be linked to China's ability to pay.

In the end, the moderate view advanced by the United States and others failed to win the day. In particular, the Germans were uncompromising in their insistence upon a heavy and punitive indemnity seeing 'no reason why the Powers should show excessive generosity in the matter'. Other influential European Powers, such as the British, ultimately bowed to the German demands out of political considerations.

In order to fix the amount of the indemnity, a committee was formed consisting of the German, French, British, and

Japanese envoys. One of the problems which the committee faced was how to find additional sources of revenue for the Manchu Government so as to ensure payment of the indemnity. The issue was a critical one because, based on information provided by the Chinese plenipotentiaries, the Imperial Government was already operating with a severe deficit. The solution eventually decided upon was to revamp China's Customs system so that additional sums could be generated from Customs revenues.

The second problem was, of course, to fix the amount of the indemnity itself. The government of each of the foreign Powers was asked to submit a list of public and private claims. Most of the figures provided by the claimants were accepted by the committee and incorporated in its report with little scrutiny. The end result, as set forth in the committee's final report, were claims totalling 462,538,116 taels. The committee's report was accepted by the Powers virtually in its entirety. As a result, the terms of the final settlement contained in the Protocol called for a lump-sum indemnity amounting to 450 million taels. In addition, interest was to be paid at the rate of 4 per cent per annum, the first payment being due on 1 July 1901. The principal amount of the indemnity was to be paid in accordance with an amortization schedule which called for the first payment due on 1 January 1902 and the last payment to be made on 31 December 1940. Both principal and interest were to be paid in gold.

Fig. 1 Rates of Exchange, 1901

| 1 tael | = | English, 3.0 shillings
German, 3.055 marks
Austro-Hungarian, 3.595 crowns
American, 0.742 dollar
French, Italian, Spanish, Belgian, 3.750 francs
Japanese, 1.407 yen
Netherlands, 1.796 florin
Russian, 1.412 gold rouble |

Fig. 2 The Public and Private Claims of the Powers, as Estimated on 1 July 1901, and as Finally Settled in the Protocol

	Estimated to 1 July 1901				Protocol Settlement	
	Public Claims		Private claims, Taels	Total Taels	Amount Taels	Per cent of whole
	National Currency	Taels				
Russia	Roubles 177,000,000	125,316,000	8,000,000	133,316,000	130,371,120	29.0
Germany	Marks 255,600,000	83,581,200	7,705,843	91,287,043	90,070,515	20.0
France	Francs 193,500,000	50,979,250	24,800,000	75,799,250	70,878,240	15.75
Great Britain	£ 6,285,933	41,839,173	9,824,856	51,664,029	50,620,545	11.25
Japan	Yen 47,574,000	33,777,540	1,775,000	35,552,540	34,793,100	7.7
U.S. America	U.S.$ 25,000,000	(Inclusive claim)		34,072,500	32,939,055	7.3
Italy	Lire 77,000,000	20,366,500	6,747,427	27,113,927	26,617,005	5.9
Belgium	Francs 31,175,000	—		8,607,750	8,484,345	1.9
Austria-Hungary	Krone 14,240,000	3,958,720	20,800	3,979,520	4,003,920	0.9
Netherlands	Florins 885,000	492,763	307,237	800,000	782,100	0.2
Spain	Pesetas 454,000	120,000	158,055	278,055	135,315	
Portugal	—	—	—	—	92,250	
Sweden	—	—	110,000	110,000	62,820	0.1
Other claims	—	—	—	—	149,670	
		Total		462,538,116	450,000,000	100.0

Source: H.B. Morse, *The International Relations of the Chinese Empire*

Having dealt with matters relating to punishment and compensation, the Protocol next turned to the issue of how to ensure that Chinese hostilities against the Powers would never recur. The first of the measures to be adopted in response to this issue was the imposition of a ban on the importation of arms and war material for a two-year period ending August 1903. Next, China was forced to agree to raze its forts at Dagu along the coast, thus preventing Chinese government forces from impeding access to, and safe exit from, Peking. In addition, the foreign Powers were granted certain rights to establish communication posts at 12 points along the railway line between Peking and the sea.

Finally, the Protocol also contained a provision explicitly recognizing the right of each of the foreign Powers to maintain a permanent military force in the capital for the protection of the Legations. Once again, a special committee was formed by the Powers to deal with this question. The proposal put forth by the British representative called for restrictions to be imposed on the military force each Power would be permitted to maintain in the capital. Under this proposal, the United Kingdom, Germany, France, Japan, and Russia would be required to limit their forces to a maximum of 200 men each. The remaining three Powers—Austria, Italy, and the United States—were to limit their forces to between 50 to 100 men each.

As usual, the strongest objections to the British proposal came from Germany, supported in this instance by Russia and Japan. The end result of the committee's deliberations was, in effect, that each of the Powers was left free to fix its own force levels based on perceived needs. These were finally agreed to be as follows:

Foreign Forces	Men	Guns	Machine-guns
Austria–Hungary	250	2 to 4	6 to 8
France	250	2	2
Germany	300	5 to 6	6
Great Britain	250	6	4 to 6
Italy	200	2	2
Japan	400	4 to 6	some
Russia	350	2	4
United States	100	2	2 to 3

It was in the context of concerns about security that the Protocol also addressed the issue of the Legation Quarter itself. Tucked in the middle of the Protocol was Article VII, which contained the following brief provision:

The Chinese Government has agreed that the Quarter occupied by the Legations shall be considered as one specially reserved for their use and placed under their exclusive control, in which Chinese shall not have the right to reside and which may be made defensible.

Simple as it was, this brief paragraph provided the legal basis for the establishment of the Legation Quarter as a separate city, walled, armed, and distant from, the surrounding city of Peking.

A portrait of the signatories of the Final Protocol of 1901.

▼

VII
Rebuilding the Legation Quarter

Rebuilding the Legation Quarter after the Siege required a tremendous effort. This photograph, taken soon after the fighting, shows much of the old Quarter in ruins. The Tartar City Wall runs diagonally from the middle of the photograph to the upper left. The road running parallel to the wall in the left hand corner of the photograph is Legation Street.

SOON AFTER THE Protocol was signed, the foreign Powers went about the task of rebuilding the Legation Quarter along the lines set out in Article VII. The first order of business was to clarify the physical limits of the new Quarter. In simplified terms, these were as prescribed by a special Annex to the Protocol: Hatamen Street on the east, Hubu Street on the west, the east end of Changan Avenue in the north and the Tartar City Wall in the south. The main effect of the extension of the Legation Quarter's boundaries was to expand the total area occupied exclusively by the Legations before the Siege nearly tenfold to more than 200 acres.

Once the outer boundaries of the new Legation Quarter had been fixed, Legation officals were keen to commence reconstruction work. Before this could be done, two tasks needed to be accomplished. Firstly, Chinese government buildings, and houses and shops owned by private citizens within the Legation area had to be removed. Secondly, the foreign Powers had to reach agreement among themselves on the size and location of their Legations and on other matters such as the setting aside of land for sale to private individuals and businesses and for common use. Since neither of these matters was dealt with in the Protocol, further negotiations were required before reconstruction of the Legation Quarter could begin.

These two photographs show the areas around Qianmen and Hatamen in the early 1900s. As a result of the Protocol, all Chinese residents were removed from the Legation Quarter and property ownership by Chinese inside the Quarter was forbidden. Chinese residents expelled from the Quarter received compensation from the Western Powers. Many Chinese took up residence in the Qianmen and Hatamen areas after their expulsion.
▼

One of the terms contained in Article VII of the Protocol, was that the new Legation Quarter was reserved for the 'exclusive use' of the foreigners. What this meant was that henceforth, no Chinese would have the right to either reside or own property in the Quarter. To implement this provision, the envoys of Austria–Hungary, Italy and France were delegated by the other Powers to develop a plan for the removal of Chinese residents and government buildings from the Quarter. The result of their work was the promulgation in 1901 of a set of 14 Articles known as the 'Regulations for the Expansion and Alteration of the Legation Quarter in Peking'. Under the Regulations, Chinese property owners in the Legation Quarter were notified to present their title deeds to the Quarter's newly-established Land Commission for registration. If the title deeds were found to be correct and genuine, they would later be returned to the owner together with a price voucher. The price voucher could be exchanged at a later date for a cash payment in an amount fixed by the Land Commission.

The implementation of the Regulations proved to be less straightforward than they appeared. It did not take long for ordinary Peking citizens to learn that money might be earned by presenting false deeds for registration. As a consequence, the process of confirming the validity of deeds became complicated and time consuming. Conflicts also arose between the foreign Powers and the Chinese authorities over the former's insistence that Chinese government buildings and temples be treated in the same manner as private property. A further source of tension was that the amount of compensation granted by the Powers under the voucher system was often quite low.

While attending to the removal of Chinese buildings and residents from the Legation Quarter, the foreign Powers seized the opportunity to expand the size of the Quarter from what had been provided in the Protocol. This was accomplished by implementing administrative rules which required that buffer areas be established along the perimeter of the outer boundaries so as to ensure that the Legation Quarter could be adequately defended against attack. Under the new regulations it was provided that all existing structures lying within the buffer areas should be pulled down and that thereafter no further buildings could be erected.

The new regulations immediately brought the Powers into conflict once again with the Chinese Government, for among the buildings earmarked for removal were a number of government buildings and imperial household shrines. In addition, the British Legation took the view that in order to effectively carry out the new rules, the Imperial City's walls opposite the north-east boundary of the Legation Quarter should be pulled down. After a long debate, various compromises were finally reached and in the end the Imperial City walls were merely lowered slightly.

The total area of the new Legation Quarter was greatly increased as a result of the re-fixing of the district's boundaries under the Protocol. At the east, the limits of the Legation Quarter touched onto Hatamen Street, which after the Siege was sometimes referred to as Kettelerstrasse. This photograph, probably taken from the top of the Tartar City Wall, shows the entrance onto Hatamen Street from the south looking north. The Legation Quarter is on the left.

The boundaries of the Legation Quarter extended to the west. This photograph, taken from the Tartar City Wall to the rear of the American Legation, looks out over Qianmen Street in the Chinese district.

Once the boundaries of the Legation Quarter had been fixed and all property inside ceded to the foreign Powers, a plan was drawn up for the reconstruction of the Quarter. As most of the buildings within the bounds of the old Legation district had been either completely destroyed or were badly damaged during the Siege, the task of reconstruction was in some ways greatly simplified. Not surprisingly, the blueprint for the reconstruction of the Legation Quarter was influenced to a large degree by concerns about security. These concerns were reflected in the first instance in the decision to erect a fortified wall which ranged between 15 to 20 feet high around the western, northern, and eastern boundaries of the Quarter, linking up on the south with the Tartar City Wall. Eight gateways, each with a massive iron gate, were set into the walls at the main points of access to and exit from the Legation Quarter. Outside the walls of the Legation Quarter on the east, west, and north was a broad open area known as the Glacis. The Glacis was the buffer area created by administrative decree. Considered as the joint property of all the foreign Legations, it was used primarily for drills and exercises by the Legation Guards.

The great Changan Avenue, or 'Avenue of Heavenly Peace', formed the northern boundary of the Legation Quarter. This photograph shows a part of the avenue to the north of the British Legation. The British renamed the street 'Stuart Road'. The western section of Changan Avenue which touched on the Italian Legation became known as the Viale Italia.

After the Siege, the size of the British Legation was increased from 12 to 36 acres. This photograph, probably taken from the roof-top of the Japanese Legation, shows the site of the British Legation about 1905. The Imperial Canal and British Legation wall are in the middle of the picture. Tiananmen, the Forbidden City, and the Western Hills are in the rear.

One of the most distinctive features of the British Legation was its entrance gate. The gate was flanked by two huge stone steps on either side which were used for mounting horses.

Canal Road ran north to south through the centre of the Legation Quarter. After the Siege, the banks of the canal were reinforced by the construction of a brick retaining wall, shown in the photograph here in front of the entrance gate to the British Legation. This section of Canal Road became known as 'British Road'. The road on the opposite side of the Canal, which fronted on the Japanese Legation, was renamed 'Meiji Road' or 'Rue Meiji'.

Inside the walls of the Legation Quarter, the map of the old foreign community was completely redrawn. Although many of the Legations remained in the same general area as they had occupied before the Siege, the size of each Legation's compound was, in almost every case, increased. Each of the new Legations surrounded itself with high stone walls behind which new Western-style buildings were constructed. A front gate, typically of impressive proportions, opened out onto the main street. Either within the grounds or adjacent thereto, each Legation maintained its own barracks for its troops, together with storehouses, stables, and other facilities.

Both because of its prominence in world affairs, and in recognition of the special role it played during the Siege, Great Britain came to occupy by far the largest area within the Legation Quarter of any of the Powers. The total size of the British Legation was increased from 12 to 36 acres, largely by expansion to the west. The new area incorporated all of the former Imperial Carriage House and most of the land which had previously been the site of the Board of War and the Board of Works. In addition, smaller parts of the old Board of State Ceremonies and the Hanlin Academy to the north were brought within the Legation's grounds. Finally, part of the old Mongol Quarter was also absorbed by the British and used as the site for the construction of barracks for its Legation guards.

The British Legation fronted to the east on to Canal Road, the avenue running along both sides of the Imperial Canal. On the British side of the canal, the road was known as 'British Road', at least until it touched the eastern end of the Russian Legation when it became once again known as Canal Road. To the north, the British also renamed the western portion of East Changan Avenue 'Stewart Road'. The former Bingbu Street, to the west of the British Legation beyond the Glacis, was given the new name 'Gaselee Road' in commemoration of the British Commander-in-Chief of the Relief Force.

The Russians had also benefited from the redrawing of the boundaries of the new Legation Quarter. The area its Legation occupied was increased nearly four times over, from a total of 5 acres to 19 acres. The southern boundary of the Legation now ran all along Legation Street from Canal Road to the edge of the Glacis, whose opposite side bordered from north to south on the Rue Linievitch, the new name given by the Russians to the southern part of the former Bingbu Street.

Running perpendicular to the north out from Legation Street was a small dead-end lane which permitted access into the Russian barracks inside the Legation grounds. After the 1917 Bolshevik Revolution, the new Soviet Government withdrew its troops from Peking and leased out most of the area to foreign residents in the Legation Quarter. The name given to the alley thereafter was 'USSR Embassy Compound Lane'.

Although Chinese were no longer permitted to reside inside the Legation Quarter, most of the reconstruction work undertaken after the Siege was performed by Chinese labourers. This photograph shows a Chinese worker rebuilding the north-east corner of the British Legation wall. Note the bullet holes and the inscription 'Lest we forget' on the wall to the rear, a reminder of the events of summer 1900.

The Protocol of 1901 allowed the foreign Powers to make the new Legation Quarter 'defensible'. Towards this end, the foreign community erected a brick wall around the perimeter of the Legation Quarter. This photograph shows the wall under construction.

▶

The American Legation also expanded its site after the Siege. The Legation eventually occupied five separate plots of land spread along Legation Street. This photograph shows the entrance gate to the Legation. A marine guard stands to the right.

Before the Siege, the American Legation occupied the site opposite the old Russian Legation. However, as the original Legation buildings were completely destroyed by the Boxers, after the Siege the US Legation took up temporary quarters in the *Sanguan Miao,** a former Buddist temple at the intersection of Legation Street and the southern part of Canal Road. Eventually, the US Legation acquired four additional plots of land, each of which was bordered by Legation Street on the north and the Tartar City Wall on the south. The site located at the western end was used as a parade ground for troops. The site to its immediate east was used for the construction of barracks to house the Legation Guards. Still moving eastwards, the next site was used for the Legation proper.

The fourth site, on which originally sat a hostel used by the Legation to house American students, was later leased to the National City Bank of New York. The site sat opposite the Russian Legation, sandwiched in between the Dutch Legation on the west and various commercial establishments and banks on the east.

* The temple played a special role in Chinese history. It is said to have been the site where the last Emperor of the Ming dynasty went to pray and seek guidance during the final hours of his reign. According to legend, as the Manchu troops surrounded the capital in 1644, the Emperor 'drew sticks' to divine the appropriate course of action. The advice was: 'commit suicide'. Soon thereafter, the Emperor hung himself.

101

Eight gateways were built into the Legation Quarter's walls providing points of entry to and exit from the Quarter. Large wrought iron gates were hung from the site towers.

The Legation Quarter's gates were manned by armed guards day and night. Chinese required a special pass to enter the Quarter.

The reconstruction of the American Legation was completed in 1905 after an appropriation by the US Congress of $60,000. As the Legation occupied more than half of the area along the Tartar City Wall from the Qianmen in the west to Canal Road in the east, the Americans were entrusted with maintaining a guard along the wall.

The Dutch Legation occupied virtually the same site as it had before the Siege. However, the area of the Legation was increased slightly to a total area of 2 acres. At one point, the refusal of the Dutch to establish a Legation Guard and assume responsibility with the Americans for protection of the Tartar City Wall in the south, led to calls by the other Powers to remove the Dutch to another location. Over time, however, these calls diminished and nothing further was done.

◄

This photograph shows an American marine guard along the western perimeter of the Legation Quarter.

▲

The Glacis—a broad open area which served as a buffer between the Legation Quarter's walls and the Chinese city—was established on the east, west and north. This picture shows a guard atop the north-eastern corner of the Legation Quarter wall looking beyond the eastern Glacis to Hatamen.

The Dutch Legation was completely rebuilt after the Siege, but it remained at the same site as it occupied during the 1800s. This photograph, taken about 1915, shows the Dutch Legation's new entrance gate along Legation Street. ►

103

At the southern end of British Road along the City Wall was the Water Gate through which the Relief Forces first entered Peking on 14 August 1900. After the Siege, the Water Gate was enlarged and made into a proper gate. This portal eventually became the main route linking the Legation Quarter and the Central Peking Railway Station, which lay just outside the City Wall.

The map of the Legation Quarter was also substantially redrawn in that portion of the Quarter which lay to the east of the Imperial Canal. One of the most important changes which occurred was the requisitioning and later razing of the Palace of Prince Su and an Imperial Ancestral Temple to make way for the new Italian Legation. In pre-Siege days the Italians had maintained their small Legation at the eastern end of the Legation Street, beyond the *Taijichang*. By moving to the new site, the Italians increased the area of the Legation from 1 acre to more than 12 acres. The Legation site now stretched from Canal Road on the west to the Rue Marco Polo on the east. To the north of the Legation the Glacis separated the Legation's walls from the East Changan Avenue which was renamed Viale Italia.

To the south of the Italian Legation, the Japanese occupied two major sites along Canal Road. Taking their cue from the British across the way, the Japanese renamed that portion of the road on which their establishment fronted, the 'Rue Meiji'. Taken together, the northern site, which encompassed the official Legation grounds, and the southern site on which the Legation barracks were built, amounted to more than 14 acres. The two sites included almost the entire southern half of the original Palace of Prince Su, which was severely damaged during the Siege. The original Legation site, consisting of slightly more than 1 acre fronting on Legation Street, was maintained as an annex.

In the centre of the Legation Quarter, along Legation Street, most of the sites originally occupied by the pre-Siege Legations remained in the hands of the original owners. The Spanish Legation, which fronted onto Legation Street, was one of the few Legation buildings left standing after the Siege. It was for this reason that it was chosen as the site for the negotiation and signing of the Protocol of 1901. As a result of the adjustments made after the Siege, the Legation grounds were increased slightly to 2 acres. As the Spanish maintained no Legation Guards, no additional land for the construction of barracks was needed.

The Glacis along the British Legation, shown in this photograph, was used as a military parade ground and polo field.

Entrance gate to the new Italian Legation, situated at the north of the Legation Quarter next to the Japanese Legation.

This photograph looks out on to the area of what is now Tiananmen Square. The Tiananmen is in the background and the western end of the Legation Quarter Glacis is on the right. The Qianmen would have stood to the rear of the photographer.

The Japanese Legation occupied two different sites, the most important being a large complex to the east of the Imperial Canal directly opposite the British Legation. This picture shows the main entrance gate to the Japanese Legation.

The Imperial Canal, which ran from north to south through the middle of the Legation Quarter, was flanked on both sides by tree-lined streets.

Legation Street during the reconstruction of the Legation Quarter.

The Central Peking Railway Station, shown in this picture, was reconstructed after the Siege on a site just outside the Tartar City Wall. The main entrance into the Legation Quarter from the railway station was through the Water Gate, which was made into a proper access way in the early 1900s.

The main entrance gate of the French Legation compound during reconstruction along Legation Street in the early 1900s. The stone lions and chain fence which appear in the photograph predate the Siege.

This photograph shows a side entrance to the Belgian Legation. The Belgians, who before the Siege occupied a site some distance from Legation Street, rebuilt their legation on land previously occupied by the palace of Xu Tong, a strong supporter of the Empress Dowager and a notorious xenophobe.

107

The German Legation, on the opposite side of Legation Street, remained at its pre-Siege site. However, the total area of the Legation grounds was increased from 2.5 acres to 25.5 acres. The Legation grounds now extended from the Hongkong Bank building on the west all the way to Rue Marco Polo on the east, interrupted in the centre by the Jardine, Matheson Peking office. Along the southern boundary of the German Legation site ran the Tartar City Wall. Like the Americans to the west, the Germans also assumed responsibility for maintaining defences along this line.

The old French Legation across the street from the Germans suffered tremendous damage during the Siege. Virtually the only objects to have emerged unharmed were the two stone lions which had been set up in front of the main gate during the 1860s. The lions remained in position after the reconstruction of the new Legation gates had been completed. The French, too, greatly expanded their Legation grounds, increasing the total area from 6 to 20 acres. The barracks for the French Legation Guards were constructed on a large plot to the east on the opposite side of the Rue Marco Polo. This new area, girded by the Rue Labrousse and the Rue Gaubil, became part of an enlarged French cultural zone. It was here, for example, that the French Club and a French school were located.

The site at the southern end of Rue Marco Polo, between the Tartar City Wall and Legation Street, was allocated to the Belgian Legation. The site was originally occupied by the palace of Xu Tong, an adviser to the Empress Dowager and a notorious leader of the anti-foreign camp at the Imperial Court. It has been said that Xu Tong's loathing for the hairy foreigners was so great that he refused to enter or exit his residence by way of the main gate which fronted on Legation Street. Instead, he chose a side door so as to avoid having to set foot on the hated foreigners' road. After the outbreak of the Siege, Xu attempted to flee from the Legation district, was detained briefly by French guards and then later released. An enthusiastic supporter of the Boxers, Xu and his entire family committed suicide in August 1900 when he learned of the arrival of the Relief forces.

Finally, in the northern sector of the Quarter, stretching from the Rue Marco Polo on the west to the Glacis on the east, was the Legation of Austria–Hungary. Before the Siege the Austrians occupied an area of something less than 2 acres.

The new site taken up by the Legation totalled approximately 10 acres.

These then were the broad outlines of the new Legation Quarter as it emerged after the signing of the Protocol of 1901. In physical terms, at least, the general setting remained largely intact right up until the 1950s. By then, however, the world—both inside and outside the Legation Quarter—had changed dramatically.

VIII

The Legations and Their World: 1901–1949

The reconstruction of the Legation Quarter in the early 1900s resulted in the creation of a miniature Western city in the heart of Peking. This photograph provides a panoramic view of the rebuilt Legation Quarter during the 1920s.

▼

THE PERIOD FROM 1901 up to the 'liberation' of Peking by Red Army troops in 1949 was one of tremendous upheaval in China. In 1908 the Guangxu Emperor died. He was followed to the grave shortly after by the Empress Dowager. Several years later, in 1911, China's moribund imperial system collapsed in the face of Sun Yatsen's revolution, and the Republic of China was established. What followed was a period of warlordism and political factionalism within, and aggression from without which culminated in the outbreak of World War II and ultimately the founding of the post-war Communist regime.

Throughout most of this period of political and social turmoil Peking's Legation Quarter grew and prospered. Its status secured by treaty obligations and the presence of foreign troops, the Legation Quarter and the foreign community which lived within its gates experienced a kind of 'Golden Age'. In this chapter we will provide a thumbnail sketch of the Legations and their world during the years following the Siege up to the establishment of the People's Republic in 1949.

The 'Europeanization' of the Legation Quarter during the earlier 1900s brought about the construction of a large number of new Western style buildings. Among the most impressive of these was the Grand Hotel des Wagons-Lits. The hotel was built at the intersection of Legation Street and Canal Street in the heart of the Legation Quarter.

▼

A City Apart

The Siege and its aftermath left much of the foreign settlement in the old *Dongjiaomin Xiang* district in rubble. The subsequent rebuilding of the foreign community during the early 1900s did not simply reconstruct the district along the old lines. Rather, as provided by the Boxer Protocol, the Powers created an exclusive foreign enclave. By the 1920s the Legation Quarter had developed into what Arlington and Lewisohn have described as 'a city quite apart and entirely different from the rest of Peking'.

The Legation Quarter's separateness from the Chinese world in its midst was defined in physical terms. First, the Quarter's new walls, barricaded gates and broad open Glacis set the Quarter at a distance from the Chinese community outside. Moreover, within the Quarter's walls, the foreign community established a 'miniature city' which recreated the world of the great foreign Powers in the centre of Peking.

As part of the plan to 'Europeanize' the Legation Quarter, efforts were made early on to improve the quality of life within the settlement. In 1902, Legation Street and the other main thoroughfares in the Quarter were widened and macadamized. At the same time, street lamps were installed. Soon thereafter an electric light company was established to supply electricity in the Quarter, and the organization of telephone, public sanitation, fire, and police services quickly followed. Later, in the mid-1920s, the Imperial Canal, its foul smell long a source of complaint, was filled in and made into a public garden planted with European flowers and shrubs and bordered by rows of comfortable benches.

The same theme of 'Europeanization' was followed in the construction of new buildings in the Quarter. Unlike the early Legations, whose premises often incorporated Chinese-style buildings converted to Western use, the new Legation buildings were designed along European lines in the appropriate national styles then in favour.

Walking along Legation Street in the 1920s had much the same effect as taking a short course in early twentieth century European architecture. As George Kates, an American who lived in Peking during the 1930s noted:

The buildings of each Legation . . . looked as if lifted bodily from their own country to be set down here in China. Not only were the styles all different, the very hardware on the windows would be

113

French, or Dutch, or British. The plumbing, the tiling, all had been transported at the expense of the State to which the building belonged, to be combined with grosser Chinese materials at hand.

The American Legation provides a good example of how each country recreated its own national world within the confines of its grey brick walls. The Legation, as described by Kates, was constructed in 'stately colonial renaissance style . . . of imported American materials, and the government architect was expressly sent to put up the Legation buildings.' The compound included a tall radio antenna for wireless transmissions, a drill ground for the Legation marines, and an indoor basketball court. The ambassador's residence was described as 'ample and comfortable'. A portrait of George Washington hung in the entrance hall next to a large grandfather clock. Less attractive were the compound buildings which housed the secretaries of the Legation. According to rumours current at the time—which have now become part of US Embassy lore—these lesser buildings were said to have been designed based on drawings for local American post offices.

The new Legations were built in Western-style architecture and usually mimicked the style then in fashion in the home country. This photograph shows a formal reception before the main building inside the French Legation. The photograph was probably taken in the 1930s.

▼

French national characteristics were also reflected in France's new Legation compound. The large entrance gates were built in neo-classical style with the letters 'RF' ('République française') placed in the centre at the top. The buildings inside were scattered about well-tended flower gardens, the overall effect being, in the words of George Kates, like some 'modern hotel delux in a French watering place'. Full of glassed-in galleries, parquet floors, and long hallways, the French Legation was even equipped with French telephones which according to Kates, 'rang with French diversity, French logic, French interruptions'.

The same rule of national replication also applied to the other Legations. In the Dutch Legation compound, the ambassador, and his staff lived in neat, red brick houses trimmed with white marble. The same design was carried over to the archway which covered the gates at the entrance. Neatness and good order prevailed, a faithful reflection of the moral values of the upright Dutch burgher.

The Japanese Legation's exterior looked like a set from some European opera—full of castellations and nooks and crannies which concealed the austere *tatami* rooms inside. It was here that on 7 May 1915, the Chinese Government was forced to accept the infamous 'Twenty-One Demands' whereby the Japanese obtained special rights over northern China.

The Belgian Legation was heavy with limestone and ornamental wrought iron. It was reportedly built according to the design of one of the Belgian king's favourite villas in the outskirts of Brussels.

The British Legation gates, the largest in the Quarter, were guarded by sentries who followed a routine which is said to have matched precisely that of their counterparts at the entrance to Buckingham Palace.

Apart from the Legations themselves, the other buildings which sprang up in the Quarter in the early 1900s completed the picture of a 'little Europe' in the Chinese capital. Foremost among the new 'commercial' buildings erected within the Quarter was the Grand Hotel des Wagons-Lits. One guest, the writer Henri Borel, described the Grand as being on the same standard as a 'Parisian hotel', fully equipped with '. . . [an] English bed with silk eiderdowns, lace curtains, a large wardrobe with mirror, electric light bulbs, a lavatory with taps for hot and cold water, a little lamp with red silk shade on a small table by the bed, a comfortable easy-chair . . .'

115

A number of Christian churches were built in Peking, but only one was constructed inside the Legation Quarter itself. This church, St. Michael's Catholic Church, was erected at the corner of Rue Marco Polo and Legation Street. It was run by the Vincentian fathers.

The Legation Quarter hosted two main hospitals, the largest and best known of which was the German hospital at the eastern end of Legation Street. The hospital was staffed by Lazarene nuns. Apart from the quality of its medical care, it was famous for the cakes and coffee which it served to its patients.

▼

The Quarter also saw the construction of a rush of new banks; several large department stores; St. Michael's Catholic Church (by the French Vincentian Fathers) at the corner of Rue Marco Polo and Legation Street; and two hospitals, one by the French at the western end of Legation Street and the other by the Germans at the eastern end of the street.

Not everyone was pleased with the Legation Quarter's new hotchpotch of European architecture. Borel, who served as a Chinese interpreter for the Dutch, rendered the following verdict after a visit in 1909: 'The entire [Quarter]...is a wretched crowd of dull buildings trying to look fine, all scrolls and bays and trivialities, all in that vile conventional modern style which causes the new portions of all European capitals to look exactly like each other.'

Chinese in the Legation Quarter

Just as the Legation Quarter became physically separate from the rest of the city of Peking, the foreign community also stood apart from the Chinese world around it. Under the terms of the Boxer Protocol of 1901, Chinese were not permitted to reside in the Quarter. Servants and other Chinese who worked inside the Legation Quarter by day were required to hold special passes which had to be presented to the Legation Guards at the entrance gates. Similarly, 'letters of introduction' were required for Chinese visitors. Over time, these strict rules were relaxed. In fact, the Legation Quarter frequently served as a place of refuge for Chinese officials and others who found themselves in political trouble outside the gates. After the fall of the Manchu dynasty, for example, many high-ranking palace eunuchs fled to the Quarter to take up temporary residence there. Later, asylum was granted to officials in t' Peking government who had fallen from grace. A former president of the Republic of China went into hiding in the Dutch Legation after the failure of his bid for power in a 1917 *coup d'état*.

Chinese who visited the Legation Quarter on business were supposed to carry 'letters of introduction' before they would be admitted.

The strict rules against Chinese taking up residence inside the Legation Quarter were relaxed from time to time. Wealthy Chinese warlords, former high-ranking eunuchs, and well-known political refugees were all granted permission to live inside the Quarter at various times. This picture shows a palace official in conversation with a Western lady at a Legation social function.

Wealthy Chinese were also apparently welcome to use the services of the foreign hospitals inside the Quarter—at least, for a price. Speaking of the German hospital during the 1930s, the American George Kates recalls that:

A war-lord could rent a suite of hospital rooms here, if he wished to retire for a temporary illness; and then delicately painted concubines, perhaps in garish satin tubular gowns recently purchased in Shanghai, caused no flurry whatever if they shuffled past on their small feet in the broad cool paved green corridors. It was even rumored that if a patient were accustomed to his daily pipe of opium, this too was conceded.

Even where there was physical proximity between Chinese and members of the foreign community, the social gulf remained. One resident of the Legation community in the early 1900s described foreigners as preoccupied with 'dinners and dancing, gossip and golf, happily ignorant of the customs or language or feelings of the people they lived among.'

Similarly, a former minister of the Italian Legation recalled his stay in Peking during 1918 as being characterized by 'a sort of diplomatic mountain fastness'. In his view, most foreigners, 'were isolated from and out of sympathy with, the country they lived in'. A foreign resident 20 years later, John Blofeld, observed that 'most inmates of the Legation Quarter led lives so detached from the currents of life swirling around them that they were always the last to know what was happening'.

The major obstacle to communication between Chinese and foreigners was, of course, linguistic. Apart from Customs officials, Legation interpreters, and missionaries, few foreigners in Peking could speak Chinese. This was as true for high-ranking members of the diplomatic corps as it was for other foreign residents. Recalling his attendance at meetings of Legation Ministers in Peking in the 1920s, a former Italian diplomat made the point quite neatly:

When we met in the British Legation in warm weather, the windows would be open on to a small inner courtyard, where the lilac blossomed in the Spring. The Legation parrot used to sit out there and join in our discussions (sometimes very aptly) with a hoarse guffaw, or a subdued chuckle, or a sudden screech. He was a talking parrot, but he only spoke Chinese, so that his remarks were unintelligible to most of the assembled diplomats.

The Foreign Community

During the first three decades of this century the population of the central urban area of Peking probably numbered between one to two million people. Of this number, it has been estimated that foreigners never exceeded more than two or three thousand. While many missionaries, Chinese-language students, and other foreigners lived throughout Peking, the highest concentration of foreign residents in the capital was within the Legation Quarter. Most of these residents were attached to one of the Legations, either as diplomats or members of the Legation Guards.

The diplomatic community represented the core of foreign society in Peking. When the Boxer Protocol was signed in 1901, 11 countries had established Legations in Peking. These included Germany, Austria–Hungary, Belgium, Spain, the United States, France, Great Britain, Italy, Japan, the Netherlands, and Russia. By 1911, Sweden, Portugal, Denmark, and Brazil had set up Legations, after entering into separate arrangements with the Chinese Government.

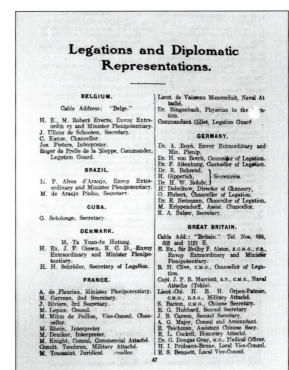

The 'official list' of the Legations and diplomatic representations in Peking taken from the Peking Who's Who *of 1922.*

119

The Bolshevik Revolution in Russia and World War I brought about further changes in the constitution of the diplomatic community. According to the *Peking Who's Who of 1922*, in that year 20 countries maintained Legations in Peking. Among the newcomers were Cuba, Mexico, Norway, Peru, the Soviet Republics and Uruguay. Austria–Hungary's Legation was abandoned after the First World War, and for a long period its building was used as an old-age hostel for foreign residents.

The diplomatic corps in Peking worked closely together on matters of common interest. Between the period of October 1890 and May 1920, members of the Legations in Peking convened 219 formal meetings to discuss issues relating to China policy. These included such items as political developments, rights and privileges of diplomatic staff, financial matters, and treaty obligations. Matters relating to the administration of the Legation Quarter itself were also frequently the subject of discussion in meetings of the diplomatic corps. Day to day

LEGATIONS AND DIPLOMATIC REPRESENTATIONS.

E. H. Brenan, Private Secretary to H.M. Minister.
A. L. Scott, Local Vice-Consul.
E. C. Mieville, Local Vice-Consul.
Major G. A. Herbert, M. C. Student Interpreter.
D. H. Clarke, Student Interpreter.
R. M. Montgomrey, Student Interpreter.
W. V. B. Hughes, Student Interpreter.
L. H. Lamb, Student Interpreter.
The Right Rev. Bishop F. L. Norris, Chaplain.
Captain Smalley, Commandant of Legation Guard.

JAPAN.
H. Ex., Y. Obata, Envoy Extraordinary and Minister Plenipotentiary.
I. Yoshida, Counsellor.
Makoto Yano, 1st Secretary.
Y. Nakahata, 3rd Secretary.
M. Yagi, 3rd Secretary.
Y. Yamara, 3rd Secretary.
S. Koga, Attaché.
E. Fukada, Attaché.
Y. Okuma, Attaché.
Y. Nezu, 2nd Secretary Interpreter.
I. Matsuura, Chancellor.
W. Kobayashi, Chancellor.
G. Sunino, Chancellor.
K. Yoshiwara, Chancellor.
H. Iwoki, Chancellor.
B. Yoshioka, Chancellor.
Maj. Gen. Otohiko Higashi, Military Attaché.
Major D. Komoto, Joint Military Attaché.
Captain C. Kita, Joint Military Attaché.
Captain S. Nakajima, Naval Attaché.
Lieut. T. Shr... a, Joint Naval Attaché.
Dr. M. Kann, Medical Officer.
T. Kimimori, Financial Attaché.
Lieut. Col. I. Hoshimura, Commandant of Legation Guard.

ITALY.
Marquis Durazzo, Minister Plenipotentiary (absent).
Vittorio Cerruti, Minister Plenipotentiary, Chargé d'Affaires.
Count L. Nani-Mocenizo, Counsellor.
Col. E. Beaud, Military Attaché.
Comt. D. Pardo, Naval Attaché.
Dr. di Giura, Medical Officer.
Rev. Pere Leonetti, Chaplain.
M. M. I. Bensa, Interpreter.
M. Ferruccio Ramondino 2nd Interpreter.
Almo Melkay, Chancellor.
Pietro Alfredo Guazzone, Secretary.

MEXICO
54, Hsin Hsien Hutung, Tel. 1165 E.
H. Ex. Dr. Don Gilberto Valenzuela, Envoy Extraordinary and Minister Plenipotentiary.
Don Pablo Herrera de Huerta, First Secretary (absent).
N. Kolessoff, Interpreter.
H. E., Sir W. J. Oudendijk, K.C.M.G.

NETHERLANDS.
(Legation des Pays-Bas).
Envoy Extraordinary and Minister Plenipotentiary.
Jonkheer J. W. C. Quarles van Ufford, Secretary.
C. G. Riem, Interpreter.
Th. H. de Josselin de Jong, Assistant Interpreter.
A. Kok, Chancellor.
Captain M. Boerstra, Military Attaché.
Captain G. J. van Loenen, Commander, Legation Guard.
E. Abell, Student Interpreter.
H. Bos, Student Interpreter.
J. van den Berg, Student Interpreter.

NORWAY.
Address: Shih Chia' Hutung.
H. E., M. Johan Michelet, Envoy Extraordinary & Minister Plenipotentiary.
Terge Knudtzou, 1st Secy., (Shanghai).

PERU.
H. E., Don Manuel de Freyre Y. Santander, Envoy Extraordinary & Minister Plenipotentiary.
Raúl A. Pinto, Secretary.

PORTUGAL
Address: Hsin Kai Lu.
H. E., Batalha de Freitas, Envoy Extraordinary & Minister Plenipotentiary.
J. Brandão Paes, Secretary and Chargé d'Affaires.
J. F. das Obagas, Secretary Interpreter.

RUSSIAN REPRESENTATIONS
MISSION OF SOVIET RUSSIA.
A. K. Paikess, Plenipotentiary Extraordinary.
D. Sandler, Secretary.

LEGATIONS AND DIPLOMATIC REPRESENTATIONS.   49

THE MISSION OF THE FAR EASTERN REPUBLIC
W. L. Pogodin, President of the Mission
A. D. Miller, Secretary.
K. A. Harnsky, Secretary.
Lt. Col. Roustam, Bok. Adviser.

SPAIN.
H. Ex. Marquis de Dosfuentes, Envoy Extraordinary and Minister Plenipotentiary.
Don Manuel Acal Y. Marin, 2nd Secretary.
Lt. Col. E. Herrerra de la Rosa, Military Attaché.
W. P. Thomas, Interpreter.

SWEDEN.
H.E. Dr. David Bergstrom, Envoy Extraordinary and Minister Plenipotentiary
Count Claes Bonde, Chargé d'Affaires.
Sven Harald Pousette, 2nd Secretary (absent).
Dr. Rutger Essen, Consul, (absent).
John Olof Zetterberg, Attaché (absent).
M. Bertil Arne Renborg, Commercial Attaché, res. at Shanghai.

UNITED STATES OF AMERICA.
J. G. Schurman, Envoy Extraordinary and Minister Plenipotentiary.
Albert B. Ruddock, 1st Secretary of Legation.
Com. C. T. Hutchins Naval Attaché.
Col. Sherwood I. Cheney, Military Attaché.
Julean Arnold, Commercial Attaché.
W. R. Peck, Chinese Secretary.
Paul B. Josselyn, Asst. Chinese Secretary.

M. A. Hofer, Second Secretary.
Jefferson Patterson, Third Secretary.
F. Finnel, Disbursing Officer.
Major J. Magruder, Asst. Military Attaché.
Major W. C. Philoon, Asst. Military Attaché.
Frank Rhea, U. S. Trade Commissioner.

Student Interpreters:
H. Bucknell.
D. C. Berger.
F. J. Chapman.
C. B. Chamberlain.
M. M. Hamilton.
G. Atcheson.
R. L. Smyth.
Edwin. F. Stanton.

Language Officers:
Major J. W. Stillwell.
Major L. P. Horsfall.
Capt. P. G. Tenney.
Major H. A. Kroner.
Lieut. A. Fisken.
Capt. N. L. Baldwin.
Capt. W. Woodbridge.
Colonel Chas. Dunlop, Commandant.

Officers of the Legation Guard:
Major Williams, U.S.M.C.
Lieutenant Commander William Chambers U.S.N.
Maj. S. Bogan, U.S.M.C.
Capt. Lott.
Captain E. B. Hammond.

URUGUAY.
Address: Tu Ti Miao Hsia Po.
Vicente Mario Carrió, Charge d'Affaires. (Shanghai).

Will newly established firms kindly communicate with the Publisher, 40 Teng Shih K'ou? :: :: :: ::

matters affecting the management of the Quarter, however, were usually handled by the Administrative Commission of the Diplomatic Quarter, a body set up in 1914. Composed of five members, three members appointed by the Diplomatic Corps and two elected by non-diplomatic establishments within the Legation Quarter, the Commission was empowered to levy taxes on the Legations and businesses in the Quarter for the maintenance of roads and bridges and the employment of policemen. Apart from providing these and other basic services, there was very little co-ordinated management of life within the Quarter. Rather, each Legation assumed responsibility for matters involving its own nationals. The result was that each of the French, Japanese, and British Legations maintained at various times their own postal service and fire services department.

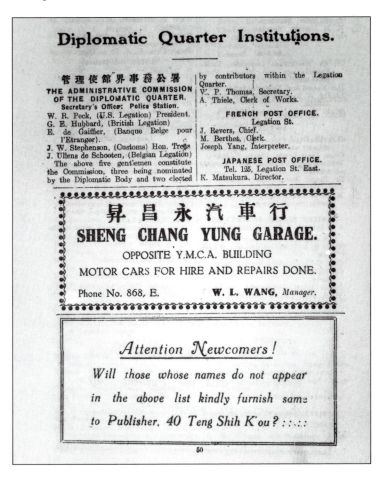

The main administrative body of the Legation Quarter was the Administrative Commission. The commission's members were listed in the Peking Who's Who. *This photograph shows the entry for the year 1922.*

In 1928 the Republican Government moved the Chinese capital to Nanjing and renamed Peking ('northern capital') to Peiping ('northern peace'). But to both the city's natives and the foreign community, Peking remained Peking. Although foreign embassies were established in Nanjing, the Legations in Peking remained the centre of foreign diplomatic activity. The Quarter retained its special status and, in fact, many diplomats continued to reside in Peking, travelling to Nanjing only when necessary.

Apart from the diplomats and their families, the military guard each Legation was permitted to maintain under the terms of the Protocol of 1901 also resided within the Legation Quarter. Over the years, however, the importance of maintaining a significant military presence in Peking gradually diminished. In 1913 the total number of guards employed by the various Legations was 2,075. By 1922 the number dropped to 997. By the time of the Japanese occupation of Peking in the late 1930s, the number of foreign troops permanently stationed in Peking had dropped even further. By then, many of the military barracks which had formally been built to house the troops had been turned over for commercial use.

The gradual reduction in the number of Legation Guards also had an impact on the status of the Glacis—the open areas on the perimeters of the Quarter originally reserved for military use. Although officially owned in common by the Legations, it was not long before individual Legations began to assert exclusive usage rights over portions of the open land. In the initial phase this was limited to the construction of sports facilities. For example, the British built their own sports and polo ground, the Italians established a Legation Athletic Club and the Americans constructed a baseball field in the Glacis. Later, building permits and leases were issued by some Legations to private companies and individuals in respect of parts of the Glacis which bordered on their Legation sites. By the late 1920s much of the Glacis was occupied by sporting facilities connected with hotels, by bars and restaurants, and by at least one licensed brothel.

The second major group of foreign residents in the Legation Quarter consisted of employees of the various Chinese Government services which were run by foreigners. These included the Imperial Maritime Customs, the Post Office, and the Salt Administration. In 1915, the Customs included more than 200 foreigners most of whom had also received their training in Chinese at the department's headquarters within the Legation Quarter. In the 1920s, 25 foreigners were employed by the Postmaster General's office in Peking, while a dozen or so worked in the Salt Administration. Most of these employees made the Legation Quarter their home.

The foreign business community made up another important group of foreign residents inside the Legation Quarter. Although Peking never rivalled the pre-eminence of Shanghai as a commercial centre, the Quarter nonetheless hosted a small business community which flourished during the first three decades of the twentieth century.

The most visible members of the foreign business community were the staff members of foreign banks. Both during the last decade of the nineteenth century and the first two decades of the twentieth, the Chinese Government's precarious financial state provided a lucrative opportunity for foreign banks. Engaged primarily in arranging loans and bond issues to finance Chinese government projects, the banks also played an important role in meeting, the financing needs of foreign companies and individual investors who were busy acquiring railroad, mining and other concessions in China during the early 1900s.

The Hongkong and Shanghai Bank was a major force in Peking in the early 1900s. During the waning days of the Chinese Empire, the Bank played an important role in providing financing to both the Chinese Government and for private investment projects. The bank's first Peking branch was built in 1885. After the Siege, new premises were built on Legation Street. This photograph shows the bank's Peking Branch in 1912.

123

One of the leaders of the banking community was the Hongkong and Shanghai Bank which had first established a branch in Peking in 1885. After the Siege the branch's premises were completely rebuilt. Completed in 1902, the bank's building was located on Legation Street next to the German Legation. The bank provided both retail banking services and acted as a liaison point between the Bank's head office and the Chinese Government. The founder of the Hongkong Bank's Peking branch and the manager of the bank for many years was Edward G. Hillier. A graduate of Trinity College, Cambridge, Hillier first took up residence in Peking in 1891. He acted for many years as the chief negotiator of the Chinese Imperial Government loans issued in London and Berlin during the years 1895 through 1905. As a result, many shared Arnot Reid's view that Hillier was regarded by many in Peking as 'perhaps the chief expert in the financial and business ways of the Chinese Government and its officials.' Blind since 1896, Hillier remained in Peking with the bank until his death in the mid-1920s.

The interior of the Hongkong and Shanghai Bank's public banking hall, about 1905.

▼

124

The Hongkong Bank's chief rival in China was the Chartered Bank of India, Australia and China. Having established its Shanghai branch in 1857, the Chartered Bank was actually the oldest established foreign bank in China. However, it did not open a branch in Peking until 1915. The bank ran its Peking operations from a specially-constructed four-storey building located at the western end of Legation Street.

▲
Edward G. Hillier served for many years as the Peking representative of the Hongkong and Shanghai Bank. Hillier lived in Peking for more than 30 years and was considered to be the leading foreign expert on Chinese financial matters.

▲
The headquarters of the Chartered Bank of India, Australia and China in Peking, circa 1907. The bank's elegant headquarters was one of the largest buildings in the Legation Quarter.

The Peking headquarters of the Yokohama Specie Bank, shown above, were located at the intersection of Legation Street and Rue Meiji, next to the Japanese Legation. ▶

Other banks which built impressive quarters on Legation Street included the Yokohama Specie Bank, located at the intersection of Legation Street and Rue Meiji; the Russo-Asiatic Bank, occupying premises on Legation Street next to the Russian (later Soviet) Legation; and the Deutsch–Asiatische Bank of Germany. The German bank's premises were located at the eastern end of Legation Street. Constructed in 1907, the new branch was built in the German style reminiscent of a Westphalian castle. For many years the branch manager was Herr Heinrich Cordes, a former diplomat with the German Legation in Peking who accompanied the German Minister, Baron von Ketteler, on the day he was murdered in 1900. Herr Cordes was succeeded in his post by his son, Herr Conrad Cordes, who remained in Peking throughout the 1920s.

Perhaps the most impressive of all the foreign banks located along Legation Street was that of the French Banque de l'Indochine et de Suez. Designed by the architectural firm of Atkinson and Dallas, Ltd., the building was constructed in 1910 in the Italian renaissance style. The main building comprised a spacious banking hall on the ground floor and the manager's private quarters on the upper floor. The roof garden

The Russo–Asiatic Bank, circa 1903.
▼

was used for entertainment. The basement housed the main vault as well as the first safe deposit boxes available for rent to private customers in Peking. Other buildings in the compound provided accommodation for the bank's foreign staff.

The Deutsch–Asiatische Bank established its Peking Headquarters, in 1907. The first manager of the Peking branch was Herr Heinrich Cordes, former aide to Baron von Ketteler who accompanied the Baron on the day he was murdered. After his retirement, Cordes was succeeded as head of the bank's Peking branch by his son.

The interior banking hall of the Deutsch–Asiatische Bank in Peking.

127

The elegant premises of the Peking branch of the Banque de l'Indochine et de Suez. The bank was constructed on Legation Street in 1910 opposite the Russian Legation.

The Peking headquarters of Jardine Matheson & Company, Ltd.

A number of trading companies established premises in the Legation Quarter. The best known is Jardine Matheson & Company, Ltd. whose presence in the Quarter predated the Siege. In 1911 Jardines built new premises in the central sector of Legation Street on a choice site adjacent to the German Legation. Jardines attended to the interests of shipping, insurance, and manufacturing firms both within China and abroad, for whom it acted as agent. Other establishments engaged in similar lines of business included the British and Chinese Corporation, Limited; Samuel & Co., Ltd.; and the Belgian Consortium des Industriels Belges en Extreme-Orient. These companies all maintained specially built premises within the Legation Quarter and played an important role in international trade and finance during the period.

The general store opened by P. Kierulff in 1874 was the first Western trading firm established in the Chinese capital. Originally opposed by the Qing Government, it soon became a favourite with Manchu princes and their ladies who spent enormous sums purchasing European curiosities such as perfume, canned food, coffee and other goods. After the Siege, Kierulff built new premises on Legation Street.

129

Apart from the 'establishment' business community of banks and major trading houses, the Legation Quarter also included a large number of stores and service trades catering to the needs of foreign residents. One of the best known shops in the Quarter was the general store of P. Kierulff & Co., which was first established in 1874. At first, the shop's opening was bitterly opposed by the Chinese Imperial Government on the grounds that the treaties permitting the establishment of the Legations did not contemplate the opening of Peking as a commercial port. Later, the Chinese relented, accepting the argument that the shop would cater only to the needs of the Legation community and would not be open to the general public. Ironically, in its early days, Kierulff's store did most of its business with Manchu nobles and court officials, who delighted in the foreign goods sold there. After the Siege, Kierulff's resumed business in new premises as general store-keeper, saddler, outfitter, silversmith, and wine and provision merchant. One of the specialities developed by the store over the years was the sale of Peking enamels, which were highly sought after in Europe during the 1920s and 1930s.

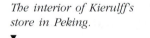

The interior of Kierulff's store in Peking.

▼

130

The Peking premises of Sennet Freres, known as 'the leading jewellers and diamond merchants of north China'.

The Regine Building provided office premises for many of the leading commercial agents of foreign businesses operating in China.

Another major trading house established in the Legation Quarter was Sennet Freres, described as 'the leading jewellers and diamond merchants of North China'. The company opened a Peking branch in 1908 at the junction of Morrison Street and the Italian Legation Glacis, with large display windows fronting on both walkways.

In addition, smaller tradesmen were in abundance: the Legation Pharmacy supplied residents with their health and pharmaceutical needs; Henri Vetch maintained a well-stocked bookshop; the French bakery offered fresh bread and cakes from its shop on Hatamen Street; photographic supplies were available from Hartung's Photo Shop; F. Ventue sold Italian wines and sweets from his shop on the Er Tiao Street inside the Quarter; and various hairdressers—most notably 'La Violette', staffed by White Russians—provided hairdressing services.

Social Life

The world of the foreign community inside the Legation Quarter was designed around Western-style comforts and entertainments. Both were provided in the first instance by the generous living conditions within the Legation compounds.

The British, occupying the largest Legation, were the leaders in providing the best facilities. Sir Meyrick Hewlitt's description of the interior of the British Legation in the early 1920s shows that, in terms of comfort at least, the British were in no way deprived:

The main building was the minister's residence, a beautiful Chinese building with an imposing entrance by a raised pathway passing under two stately porticos, known in Chinese as *t'ing'rh*. All these were covered with the official green tiles, permitted only to officials of high rank, yellow being reserved for the imperial palace. The secretaries were housed in bungalows, with the exception of the first Secretary who had a foreign-style two-storeyed house. The students and chancery assistants were located in three sets of buildings: the Escort Quarters, a two-storeyed building in Chinese style; the Stable Quarters, a two-storeyed foreign building in the stables; and the Students' Quarters, a long two-storeyed building also in foreign style. There was also a chapel, a theatre and a bowling alley.

Several decades later, an American visitor to the British Legation gave the following description of the interior:

There were well-maintained and comfortable small houses, glossily painted, with small parlors and small stairs, tiled huts and much chintz, good books and cheerful fires, rear gardens and stables, all clustered about the ambassador's much larger residence. . . . The dinners there, if not the most interesting gastronomically, were the most formal and of course the best served.

In comparison with the British Legation, the Italian Legation compound would likely have been seen as a distinctly second-class establishment. Yet, the Legation compound included a minister's residence, a separate house for the Legation's First Secretary and various other out-buildings. Mr Daniele Varé, who served as First Secretary in the Italian Legation in 1913, described the compound as including the following:

A chapel (as big as most churches) with a ceiling that had been sent out from Italy; stables for 18 horses, with exercise grounds and a large stable yard. A washhouse, a water tower, hothouses and two little buildings for the Chinese servants, the whole enclosed in a large shady garden. Besides all this, and connected with the Legation compound, were barracks for the naval guard, with hospital, kitchens, houses for officers and petty officers; restrooms, offices, a prison and a munitions depot. Also a building housing apparatus to distill water and more stables.

Nor was there apparently any shortage of servants within the Legation compounds. Again, Mr Varé noted in his memoirs that he had 10 household servants for his personal use. In addition, the Legation employed various stablemen and grooms, washermen, gardeners, gate porters, letter carriers, and others.

Foreigners within the Legation Quarter were obliged to create their own amusement. As was the case before the Siege, dinner parties, dances, and picnics led the list of the most popular amusements. Entertainment and fellowship was also available in a wide variety of other forms. A listing of the 'Clubs and Societies' in the *Peking Who's Who of 1922* includes the following:

Albion British Tennis Club
Alliance Française
American Chamber of Commerce
Ancient and Accepted Scottish Right
British Women's League
Chinese Social and Political Science Association

Choral Society
Christian Fellowship
Friday Study Club
Mothers' Club
Peking Golf and Country Club
Peking British Chamber of Commerce
Peking Club
Peking International Amateur Dramatic Club
Peking Race Club
Peking Club Hockey Club
Peking Polo Club
St. Andrew's Society
Things Chinese Society
Friends of Literature Society

In addition, Legation Quarter residents continued their habit of taking up residence in the western hills 12 miles to the west of Peking during the hot summer months. In these pleasant surroundings, many Legations and business establishments purchased old Buddhist temples and converted them for use as private bungalows. The American diplomat, Charles Denby, wrote fondly: 'Life at the hills was unsurpassed in its comfort and enjoyment. For once etiquette was done away with. Everybody dressed in white linen. The evening coat was tabooed. Excursions and picnics were the order of the day.' Apparently, as regards sartorial matters, 'everybody' did not include the British. The British Minister in Peking from 1906–20, Sir John Newall Jordan, GCIE, KCB, KCMG, reportedly dressed in a dinner jacket during his summer-time visits to the hills— even when he dined alone!

For most, the western hills were the place to unwind and escape the tensions of ordinary life in Peking, and it was not long before the foreigners made the hills their own. In addition to renovating the interior of the temples to conform to Western notions of style, they also gave foreign names to many of the geographical features in the surrounding countryside. For example, Qingshan became known as 'Burlinggame Mountain' after the first American envoy. Similarly, Hutou Shan was renamed 'Mount Bruce' after the first British envoy.

In addition to a special fondness for their retreats in the hills, the foreign community keenly pursued the sport of horse racing. A *paumachang*, or horse-race track, was first

The Peking races were immensely popular with both foreign residents of the Legation Quarter and invited Chinese guests. Shown here is the Peking race track in the late 1920s. The original grandstands, built in 1863, were burnt to the ground during the Siege.

established in 1863 on a site a little more than four miles from Peking. The grandstand was burnt to the ground during the Siege, but was rebuilt on a grander scale later. Apart from several years following World War I, the races ran uninterrupted until 1937. During the racing season, special trains brought spectators from the Legations to the track on Fridays and Saturdays. Although the Peking track did not attract the vast sums of money which one saw at Shanghai and Tianjin, it was nonetheless wildly popular with both foreigners in the Legations and Chinese alike.

The automobile came to Peking in the 1920s. Automobile excursions from the Legation Quarter to the Summer Palace outside the city were extremely popular.

Tourism became popular in Peking in the 1920s and 1930s. Many foreign tourists who visited the city, camera in hand, stayed at one of the hotels in the Legation Quarter.

With the extension of the railway lines from Peking, and the coming of automobiles to China in the 1920s, excursions farther afield provided another popular diversion. For example, it was during this period that weeked trips to the. Great Wall, the Ming Tombs, and the Summer Palace became *de rigueur* for foreign residents. Improved transport also allowed many members of the foreign community to spend summer at the northern seaside resort of Beidaihe or in the German concession area of Qingdao in Shandong.

Peking Personalities: A Short Album

For many foreigners Peking was merely a temporary assignment. For others, the city became home. Whatever the case, Peking and the Legation Quarter attracted a number of fascinating, and sometimes eccentric, personalities.

One of the most eminent of the Quarter's early foreign residents was Sir Robert Hart, a native of Northern Ireland who served from 1863 through 1911 as Inspector General of the Chinese Imperial Maritime Customs Service. Fluent in Chinese, which he reportedly spoke with a heavy Irish accent, Hart ruled the Service with an iron fist. Autocratic, egotistical and difficult, Hart was nonetheless a legendary figure in Peking even during his own lifetime. With broad contacts throughout the Chinese and foreign communities, Hart acted as advisor to both the Manchu court and the foreign Powers. He was also well-known as 'a lady's man' and a musician. His private brass band made up of local Chinese performers often provided the main entertainment at Legation social functions.

Hart lived in China for nearly 50 years and was clearly spellbound by what *The Times* called 'that strange fascination which a Chinese environment so often exercises over the European mind.' Despite his knowledge of China and his broad contacts, he failed to predict the Siege and was shocked by its destruction. He returned to England, disillusioned, in 1908 and died three years later.

Sir Robert Hart's period of residence in Peking coincided with that of Auguste Chamot, the Swiss proprietor of the original Hôtel de Pékin, and his American wife. Known throughout the Legation community as the best Western chefs in Peking, the Chamots distinguished themselves by their bravery during the Siege. Their hotel completely destroyed by Boxer fire, the

▲
Sir Robert Hart, the Inspector General or 'IG' of the Chinese Imperial Maritime Customs Service.

couple refused to retreat to the British Legation for safety but remained outside manning the defences. Later, during the aftermath of the Siege, both husband and wife reportedly earned a fortune from the sale of antiques and jewellery acquired during their looting sprees. In the early 1900s they left Peking to retire in San Francisco. Soon after their arrival, however, they lost everything in the 1906 earthquake. The couple were divorced shortly afterwards. Mr Chamot died in poverty at age 43, having married his mistress on his death bed.

Another well-known Peking resident was Dr George E. Morrison, later known as 'Morrison of Peking'. Born in Australia in 1862, Morrison arrived in China in 1894 and proceeded to walk, unarmed, from Shanghai to Rangoon. In 1897 he was appointed the Peking correspondent of *The Times* of London, a post which he held until 1912. Although he never learned to either read or speak Chinese, Morrison was nonetheless widely viewed as Europe's foremost 'China expert' at the time. In 1912, Morrison left journalism to accept an appointment as advisor to the then President of the new Republic of China, Yuan Shikai. He quickly became disillusioned, however, and later resigned. Morrison left Peking in 1918 and died in London two years later. Today's famed *Wangfujing* Street was named Morrison Street in 1920 in his honour, a designation which remained until 1949.

Willard D. Straight (1880–1918) was a major figure in the foreign business community in Peking during the waning years of the Manchu dynasty. An American who served under Sir Robert Hart in the Customs Service from 1901–5, Straight later took up diplomatic posts in Shenyang and Washington before returning to Peking in 1909. During the next three years Straight acted as lead negotiator for a group of American banks and other investors in connection with various railroad and mining concessions. Straight later returned to the US, where he became associated with J.P. Morgan and Company and founded the liberal publication, *The New Republic*.

Straight was a central player in the political machinations which led to the participation by American banks in the international consortium which provided the Hukuang railway loan of 1911. The loan was used to finance the construction of a major rail line linking north and south China. To repay the loan the Imperial Chinese Government issued bonds, which were ultimately placed with investors throughout the world.

The Chinese Government ceased payments under the bonds in the 1930s. Straight and the Hukuang bond affair became the subjects of considerable controversy in the early 1980s when a group of American bond-holders sued the Government of the People's Republic of China—the 'successor' to China's Imperial Government—for repayment in US court. The lawsuit caused severe tensions in Sino–US relations, and China at first refused to accept the US court's jurisdiction over it. Later, Straight's diaries about the circumstances surrounding his negotiations in the Legation Quarter during 1909–11 provided important information for China's ultimately successful defence in the case, led by American lawyers Eugene Theroux and Thomas Peele.

Perhaps the most colourful, if not bizarre, of Peking's foreign residents was Sir Edmund Trelawny Backhouse. An English baronet, Backhouse arrived in Peking in 1897 to take up a post in the British Legation. He quickly acquired a remarkable facility in spoken and written Chinese and was frequently sought after as an interpreter. Backhouse served for a time as an assistant to Morrison, survived the Siege by taking refuge in the British Legation, and was briefly arrested during the post-Siege days for 'blackmailing, looting and robbery'. Apart from acquiring a small fortune in cash, jewellery, and antiques, Backhouse amassed a large collection of Chinese books and manuscripts, which he later donated to the Bodleian Library at Oxford. After the Siege, Backhouse collaborated with another Englishman, W.O. Bland, in writing *China Under the Empress Dowager* (1910) and other books which were purportedly based on the secret diaries of Manchu court officials. A well-known figure in Peking, Backhouse later grew increasingly withdrawn from the foreign community. He moved out of the Quarter into a Chinese house, grew a long beard and stopped wearing Western clothing in favour of the silk gown of a Chinese scholar. After the Japanese invasion of Peking, Backhouse lived for a time in the old Austrian Legation. Although British nationals were interned after the outbreak of World War II, Backhouse was given special permission to remain in Peking. He died in a room in the French Hospital in 1941.

Many years later documents which purport to be Backhouse's private papers came to light. Among them was a work entitled 'Décadance Mandchoue'. Apart from calling into question

An early photograph of Sir Edmond Trelawny Backhouse, before he took to wearing Chinese gowns and before he grew his long scholar's beard. Backhouse was unmasked as a fraud and master forger by the British historian, Hugh Trevor-Roper, in his 1976 study Hermit of Peking: The Hidden Life of Sir Edmund Backhouse.

the authenticity of many of the Chinese sources used in his scholarly work (they may have been forged by Backhouse himself), the papers describe the seamier side of Peking's lurid nightlife in the early to mid 1900s and the 'hidden life' led by Backhouse during the period. Among the many rumours which swirled about the Legation Quarter during his lifetime was that Backhouse, fluent in Manchu as well as Chinese, was the secret lover of the Empress Dowager.

Shadows on the Legations

The exclusive world of the foreign Legations in Peking did not endure. Shadows began to fall on the foreign city within the Chinese capital in 1937. In that year the Japanese entered Peking and imposed a brutal occupation which lasted until the spring of 1945.

For most foreigners in the Legation Quarter life did not change immediately with the coming of the Japanese. However, by 1941, with the entry of America in World War II, most Westerners were considered 'alien enemies'. Many foreigners had already left Peking by then, and of those who remained most, (except nationals of the Axis Powers), were interned by the Japanese.

The defeat of Japan in 1945 failed to restore the pre-war way of life. The civil war between the Nationalist Government and the Chinese Communists resumed, bringing in its wake economic chaos, political terror, and spiritual exhaustion. By 1949, when the Red Army seized control over the capital, most foreigners knew that the die had been cast.

IX

Postscript

◀

The entrance gate to the old Austro–Hungarian Legation. After World War I, the Legation buildings were leased out to tenants. In 1940 it became the German Social Club. The Hungarian People's Republic used the old Legation as its embassy from 1949–69. Today the compound houses several Chinese research institutes.

ON 1 OCTOBER 1949 the People's Republic of China was formally established. Earlier that day at the celebrations which took place before the Tiananmen Gate in central Peking, Mao Zedong declared that 'the Chinese people had now stood up'. His words were probably not audible in the tree-lined streets of the Legation Quarter nearby. Still, there could have been little doubt among the foreign residents of the Quarter that day that the privileged world of the Legations would soon cease to exist.

Soon after the 'liberation' of Peking, the Communist authorities went about dismantling the legal and political arrangements which provided the basis for the special status enjoyed by the Legation Quarter and its residents. In the months and years that followed, the character and appearance of the old Quarter was thoroughly transformed.

Early on, foreign businesses and shops were closed and missionaries were expelled. All of the foreign street names were removed and the old Chinese names restored. The gates and towers providing access to the Quarter were demolished, and the walls surrounding the area were pulled down. The eastern Glacis, which once echoed with the sounds of foreign troops at drill practice, was made into a 'People's Park' with artificial mountains and Chinese-style pavilions.

The site of the old 'Imperial Canal' is today a park. Zhengyi Lu, or 'Righteousness Road', has now replaced the old 'British Road' and 'Rue Meiji' street signs.

142

Up until the late 1950s, the Legation Quarter retained its principal function as a place for the residence of foreign diplomats. However, the political landscape of the new Quarter—like that of the post-1949 world—had changed. Countries which had failed to immediately recognize the new Chinese People's Government had their Legation premises confiscated. Most of these, such as the American, French, and British Legations, were subsequently converted into guest-houses by the Ministry of Foreign Affairs. The German Democratic Republic (East Germany) took over the German Legation premises, Burma was assigned the premises of the former Belgian Legation, and the Hungarian People's Republic succeeded to the former Legation of Austria–Hungary.

The Spanish Legation's entrance gate is all that remains today. The buildings where the Protocol of 1901 was negotiated and signed have long been torn down.

Other Legation compounds and buildings in the Quarter were put to new use by the Chinese. For example, the former Spanish Legation, whose building pre-dated the Siege, was made the headquarters of the Diplomatic Service Bureau, the Chinese State-owned company which provides services to foreign diplomats in Peking. The old Grand Hotel des Wagons-Lits was turned into a guest-house for visiting cadres from the countryside and later a dormitory for Foreign Ministry personnel.

Along the eastern end of Legation Street, now once again known as the *Dongjiaomin Xiang*, the old German Legation barracks were razed to make way for the construction of the

Xinqiao Hotel, a huge Soviet-style concrete and brick edifice. On the *Taijichang* Street, formerly Rue Marco Polo, opposite the old Peking Club, a new building was put up to house the Central Committee of the Peking Communist Party. The Japanese Legation was taken over in its entirety to serve as the headquarters of the Peking Municipal People's Government.

The old entrance gate to the Japanese Legation, now the Peking Municipal People's Government.

The old Peking Club, now used by high-ranking Chinese Communist Party officials.

144

Beginning in 1958, the Chinese authorities set about removing foreign diplomats to a new embassy district on the other side of Peking. By the start of the Cultural Revolution (1966–76) the process was complete. As a result, the Legation Quarter had ceased entirely to be a place of residence for foreigners. During the turmoil of the Cultural Revolution, the old Legation Quarter was a favourite target for the Red Guards. Legation Street was once again renamed, this time as 'Anti-Imperialism Street'. Anything that spoke too kindly of foreign culture or stood as a reminder of past foreign influence was attacked, defaced or destroyed.

Reports by visitors to Peking in the early 1970s indicate that St. Michael's Church, at the intersection of the old Legation Street and Rue Marco Polo, was apparently a frequent target of such attacks. Most of its stained glass windows were destroyed, its bell was removed, and its stone spires partly dismantled. A magnificent hand-made pipe organ, which had not been played since 'liberation', disappeared. The metal cross at the front of the facade was bent back and twisted to one side.

St. Michael's Church, built in 1902, was a target of Red Guard attacks during the Cultural Revolution. It was renovated by the Chinese Patriotic Catholic Church in December 1989 and re-named the Dongjiaomin Xiang *Catholic Church.*

In the early 1980s the physical outlines of the old Legation Quarter were still recognizable. Moreover, many of the Quarter's best known buildings along Legation Street were still standing, but were now transformed.

The old French Hospital at the western end of *Dongjiaomin Xiang* was converted to provide offices for the People's Procuracy and for a local law firm dealing mainly with criminal matters. The Chartered Bank's old headquarters next door were made into a guest-house for the Public Security Bureau. The beautiful colonnaded building which was once the Peking office of the first National City Bank of New York was taken over by the Peking Municipal Fire Department, as was the magnificent Banque de l'Indochine next door.

The First National City Bank's branch on Legation Street is now the headquarters of the Peking Fire Department.

146

The old Banque de l'Indochine et de Suez building on Legation Street, now used by the Peking Fire Department.

For many years, the stately buildings of the Russian Legation were used by the Chinese Supreme People's Court and Procuracy. The old buildings were razed in the mid-1980s to make way for a new, modern court building. However, the old Russian Legation gates remain. Through them now pass Chinese officials hidden behind drawn curtains covering the windows of Mercedes-Benz sedans and ordinary Chinese passing through on foot, petitions in hand.

The buildings which once housed the Grand Hotel des Wagons-Lits, the Peking headquarters of Jardine, Matheson & Co. and the Hongkong and Shanghai Bank were all still standing in the early 1980s. But by 1986 they too had been knocked down. The premises of Jardine, Matheson and the bank were forced to give way to more immediate needs: the Capital Hotel, owned by China's State-run tourism authority. The site once occupied by the Grand Hotel was, in early 1992, still an empty lot.

Further north, the Chinese Maritime Customs compound and the Italian Legation became the headquarters of the Chinese People's Friendship Association. In addition, several residences in the compound have from time to time been reserved for use by 'foreign friends' who supported the Chinese revolution and ultimately acquired Chinese citizenship. Two well-known former residents of the compound in the 1950s and 1960s were the American writer Anna Louise Strong, and the New Zealander, Rewi Alley. The old British Legation, now opening out on the *Zhengyi Lu,* or 'Righteousness Road', was taken over by the Ministry of Public Security. The imposing entrance gate still remains, but it is now permanently locked. The stone-hewn steps on opposite sides of the gate—used to facilitate mounting a horse or a carriage—are also still in place, laying forlornly on their sides.

Many other Legation buildings are used as official guest-houses under the Ministry of Foreign Affairs, the modern-day successor to the old Zongli Yamen. For example, the old Austro-Hungarian Legation now houses the Institute of International Studies. The main gates and split centre stairway in the Chancellery Building are original. The building was used as the site for the 1984 Sino–British talks on the future of Hong Kong. The French Legation has for many years served as the Peking residence of Prince Sihanouk of Cambodia. In the mid-1970s the main house in the compound was pulled down to make way for a 'mini-palace' for the Prince. Its architectural design is a bizarre mixture of Chinese socialist, French colonial, and south-east Asian styles.

The entrance gate to the former French Legation as it looks today. Prince Sihanouk's Peking villa is to the rear, behind the ornamental Chinese garden.
▼

The entrance to the old Dutch Legation on Legation Street has now been bricked up.

The Deutsch-Asiatische Bank's building was used in recent years as the set for Chinese horror films. It has long been unoccupied and was pulled down in January 1992. This picture was taken several weeks before its destruction.

One of the side entrances to the old German Legation, now a dormitory and meeting place of the Ministry of Foreign Affairs.

Other Legation buildings have been rented out to foreign firms for use as residential and office premises. For example, the Bank of America established its Peking representative office in the early 1980s in the old American Legation compound. As new office buildings were opened in Peking in the mid-1980s, however, fewer and fewer of the old Legations were being occupied by foreigners. Some have now been taken up by Chinese firms. For example, the old Yokohama Specie Bank now serves as headquarters for a Chinese financial institution. The former Deutsch-Asiatische Bank building at the eastern end of Legation Street was used as a set for Chinese horror films until it was pulled down in January 1992.

For the most part, even when occupied, the old buildings still standing in the Legation Quarter have been neglected, left to fend for themselves. The one notable exception is St Michael's Church, which was partially restored (except for the bell and organ) and reopened in 1989. The church aside, the Chinese authorities have shown little interest in the preservation of the buildings formerly occupied by the Legations and proposals by foreigners in the early 1980s to refurbish part of the old Quarter for use as a foreign residential area were politely declined. As the years go by, more and more of the old buildings crumble, and are removed and replaced by 'modern' concrete-slab high-rises. Within the next five years, most of the old Quarter will probably have vanished forever.

The old Legation Quarter post office on Legation Street was used as the local People's Post Office until only recently. ▶

▲

The once imposing entrance gate to the British Legation. Today the gates are permanently shut.

Of course, it should come as no surprise that the Chinese would be reluctant to preserve the Legation Quarter. For them, it is a symbol of China's humiliation at the hands of the foreign Powers. Even today, walking down the streets of the Legation Quarter, past the now dilapidated buildings, recalling in one's imagination the diplomatic corps at table, the cozy clubs, and the foreign soldiers at the gates, one can sense how the residents of Peking must have felt about this 'city within a city', a community which was part of, yet arrogantly set apart from, the Chinese world of Peking.

The eminent historian H.B. Morse was not far from the mark when he wrote more than seventy years ago:

The Legation Quarter may be considered as the provision of a defensible fortress in the heart of the capital of a hostile Power—for which purpose it was much too large; or as the happy grasping of the opportunity to provide spacious quarters for the diplomatic representatives of the Powers, in park-like surroundings, free from the old-time insanitary conditions, and at the cost of China—and in that case it was not justified.

151

Glossary of Chinese Terms

Pinyin	Traditional Romanization	Chinese Characters
Beijing	Peking	北京
Beitang	Pei T'ang	北堂
Dagu	Ta ku	大沽
Dongjiaomin Xiang	Tung Chiao Min Hsiang	东郊民巷
Guangzhou	Canton	广州
Hatamen	Ha Ta Men	哈德门
Hanlin Yuan	Han Lin Yuen	翰林院
hutong	*hu-t'ung*	胡同
Jiangmi Xiang	Chiang Mi Hsiang	江米巷
koutou	*k'ow tow* (or *kow tow*)	叩头
Nantang	Nan T'ang	南堂
Qianmen	Ch'ien Men	前门
Sanguan Miao	San Kuan Miao	三官庙
Shuiguan	Shui Kuan	水关
Siyiguan	Szu Yi Kuan	四夷馆
Suwangfu	Su Wang Fu	肃王府
Taijichang	T'ai Chi Ch'ang	台基厂
Tianjin	Tientsin	天津
Wangfu	Wang Fu	王府
Yihequan	I Ho Ch'uan	义和拳
Yühe	Yü Ho	御河
Zhongguo	Chung Kuo	中国
Zongli Yamen	Tsung Li Yamen	总理衙门

Bibliography

Allen, Revd Roland, *The Siege of the Peking Legations* (London, 1901).

Arlington, L.C. and Lewisohn, W., *In Search of Old Peking* (Peking, 1935; Reprinted in Hong Kong by Oxford University Press, 1987).

Bland, J.O.P., and Backhouse, E., *China Under the Empress Dowager* (London, 1911).

Blofeld, John, *City of Lingering Splendour* (Boston, Shambhala Press, 1989).

Bodde, Derk, *Peking Diary: A Year of Revolution* (New York, Abelard-Schuman, 1950).

Borel, Henri, *The New China, A Traveller's Impressions* (London, 1912).

Bredon, Juilet, *Sir Robert Hart* (London, 1909).

—— *Peking* (Shanghai, Kelly and Walsh, 1919).

Bridge, Ann, *Peking Picnic* (Boston, Little, Brown & Company, 1932).

Brown, Revd Frederick, *From Tientsin to Peking with the Allied Forces* (London, 1902).

Cameron, Nigel, *Barbarians and Mandarins* (Hong Kong, Oxford University Press, 1989).

Casserly, Captain Gordon, *The Land of the Boxers* (London, 1903).

Chirlol, Valentine, *The Far Eastern Question* (London, 1898).

Coates, Austin, *China Races* (Hong Kong, Oxford University Press, 1983).

Coltman, Revd R., *Beleaguered in Peking* (Philadelphia, 1901).

Conger, Sara Pike, *Letters From China* (London, 1909).

Cook, *Cook's Guide to Peking* (1924).

Cook, Thomas & Son, *Peking and the Overland Route* (London, Thomas Cook & Son, 1917).

Denby, Charles, *China and Her People* (Boston, L.C. Page & Co., 1906), Vols. 1 & 2.

Edkins, J., *Description of Peking* (1898).

—— *Recent Changes at Peking* (1902).

Feuerwerker, Albert, *The Foreign Establishment in China in the Early Twentieth Century* (University of Michigan, 1976).

Fleming, Peter, *The Siege At Peking* (Hong Kong, Oxford University Press, 1983).

Gilbert, Peter, *China, Early Western Contacts to 1911* (Australian National University Press, Canberra, 1982).

Happer, Revd A. P., *A Visit to Peking* (1879).

Hewlett, W. Meyrick, *The Siege of the Peking Legations* (Harrow-on-the-Hill, 1900).

—— *Forty Years in China* (London, 1943).

Hooker, Mary, *Behind the Scenes in Peking* (London, 1910).

Japanese Government Railways, *Guide to China* (Tokyo, Japanese

Government Railways, 1924).

Kaminski, Gerd and Unterrieder, Else, *Von Oesterreichern und Chinesen* (Vienna, Europa Verlag, 1980).

Kidd, David, *Peking Story, The Last Days of Old China* (New York, Clarkson N. Potter, 1988).

Keats, George, N., *The Years That Were Fat, Peking 1933–1940* (New York, Harper & Brothers Publishers, 1952).

Landor, Henry Savage, *China and the Allies*, 2 Vols. (London, 1901).

Little, Mrs. Archibald, *Guide to Peking* (Tientsin, Tientsin Press, 1904).

—— *Round About My Peking Garden* (1905).

Lynn, J.C.H., *Social Life of the Chinese in Peking* (1928).

Mennie, D., *The Pageant of Peking*, (1924).

Michie, Alexander, *The Englishman in China during the Victorian Era* (Edinburgh and London, William Blackwood & Sons, 1900).

Morrison, Hedda Hammer, *A Photographer in Old Peking* (Hong Kong, Oxford University Press, 1985).

Morse, H.B., *The International Relations of the Chinese Empire*, 3 Vols. (London, Longmans, 1910–1918).

Norman, H., *The Peoples and Politics of the Far East* (New York, 1895).

Olphant, N., *A Diary of the Siege of the Legations in Peking* (London, 1901).

The Peiping Chronicle, *Guide to Peking* (Peiping, The Peiping Chronicle, 1935).

Perckhammer, Heinz von, *Peking—Das Gesicht der Stadte* (Berlin, Albertus-Verlag, 1928).

Quennel, Peter, *A Superficial Journey Through Tokyo and Peking* (London, Faber & Faber, 1932, Oxford reprint, 1986).

Ramsay, Alexander, *The Peking Who's Who 1922* (Peking, 1922).

Reid, Arnot, *From Peking to Petersburg* (London, Edward Arnold & Co., 1899).

Reinsch, Paul, *An American Diplomat in China* (1922).

Rennic, D.F., *Peking and the Pekinese During the First Year of the British Embassy in Peking* (London, 1865).

Savage-Landor, A.H., *China and the Allies* (London, 1901).

Scheibert, J., *Der Krieg In China* (Berlag Von Schroder, Berlin, 1901).

Smith, Arthur H., *China in Convulsion*, 2 Vols. (New York, 1901).

Swallow, R.W., *Sidelights on Peking Life* (1927).

Trevor-Roper, Hugh, *Hermit of Peking, The Hidden Life of Sir Edmund Blackhouse* (London, McMillan Publishers Limited, 1976).

Van Den Berg, Mieke, 'Brief Information for Legation Quarter Walk' (unpublished manuscript).

Vare, Daniele, *Laughing Diplomat* (New York, Doubleday & Co., 1938).

Waldersee, Alfred, Count von, *A Field-Marshall's Memoirs* (London, 1924).

Weale Putnam, B.L., *Indiscreet Letters From Peking* (London, 1906).

Willoughby, *Foreign Rights And Interests In China*, 2 Vols. (Baltimore, Johns Hopkins Press, 1927).

Wright, Arnold, *Twentieth Century Impressions of Hong Kong, Shanghai, etc.* (London, 1908).

Chinese Books

Beijing Wangshitan [*Talks on Peking of the Past*] (Beijing Publishing House, 1986).

Zhou Shibi, *Gu Jin BeiJing* [*Peking Today and Yesterday*] (Peking, China Chan Wang Publishing Co., 1982).

Beijing Shi [Peking History] (Peking, Beijing Publishing House, 1985).

Beijing Diming Mantan [*Talks on Place Nsames in Peking*] (Peking, Beijing Publicity House, 1990).

Beijing Jiuying [*Old Photos of Beijing*] (Peking, People's Arts Publishing House, 1989).

Index

Alexander I, Tsar, 5
Alley, Rewi, 147
Allied Expeditionary Force, 70, 76, 80
Amherst, Lord, 5
Arrow (Chinese attack on), 8

Backhouse, Sir Edmund Trelawny, 138
Bank of America, 150
Banque de l'Indochine et de Suez, 126, 128, 146–7
Beau, Paul, 82
Belgian Consortium des Industriels Belges
   en Extreme–Orient, 129
Bingbu Street, 19, 99
Bland, W.O., 138
Blofeld, John, 118
Board of Astronomy, 19
Board of Civil Affairs, 19
Board of Medicine, 19
Board of Revenue, 19
Board of Rites, 19
Board of State Ceremonies, 19, 99
Board of War, 19–20, 99
Board of Works, 19–20, 99
Borel, Henri, 115–6
British and Chinese Corporation, Ltd., 129
Brooks, S.M., 49–50
Boxers, 41, 44–54, 56, 58–61, 65, 67, 70–2, 75,
   86–8, 101, 108
Boxer Siege of 1900, 18–19, 21, 26, 37, 41–2, 52,
   59, 60–2, 65–7, 69–72, 74, 76–80, 82, 87–8, 93–4,
   96–104, 107–8, 112, 124, 129–130, 135–8, 143
British Road, 98–9, 104, 142
Bruce, Mr Frederick, 1, 10, 14
Bruce, Lord James, the Eighth Earl of Elgin, 8–11, 19
Burlingame, Mr Anson, 14

Canal Road, 98–9, 101–2, 104, 112
Canal Street, 64
Canton system, 5–6
Central Peking Railway Station, 104, 107
Chamot, Auguste, 37, 51, 136, 137
Changan Avenue, 20, 25, 94, 96, 99, 104
Chartered Bank of India, Australia and China, 125, 146
Chinese Christians, 47, 49, 54, 58, 59, 61
Chinese Imperial Observatory, 78
Cologan, B.J. Day, 82
Convention of Peking, 11, 13, 15, 19
Cordes, Herr Conrad, 126–7

Cordes, Herr Heinrich, 55, 126–7
Customs Street, also see Rue Marco Polo, 25, 31

De Balluseck, General L., 14
De Bourboulon, Monsieur, 1, 10, 14
De Giers, M., 82
Denby, Charles, 34, 36, 134
Deutsch-Asiatische Bank (of Germany), 126–7, 149,
   150
Diplomatic Corps, 36, 51–2, 54–5, 79, 118, 120–1,
   151
Diplomatic Quarter (Administrative Commission of),
   121
Duke of Liang, 20–1
Dutch East Indies Company, 4

Eastern Lane of the Mingling of Peoples
   (Dongjiaomin Xiang), *also see* Legation Street, 13,
    16–8, 42, 113, 143, 145–6
Emperor Daoguang, 8
Emperor Guangxu, 45, 112
Emperor Kangxi, 21
Emperor Qian Long, 5
Empress Dowager, 42, 44–5, 52, 70, 82, 83, 86,
   107–8, 112, 139
Enhai, 57
Eulenburg, Graf, 14

Favier, Monsignor, 50–1, 67
First Opium War, 8
Four Barbarians Hostel, (Siyiguan), 16

Glacis, 97, 99, 103–5, 108, 113, 122, 132, 142
Glutinous Rice Lane (Jiangmi Xiang), 16
Gros, Baron, 20

Hague, 88
Hall of Ceremonies (Li Bu), 11
Hart, Sir Robert, 61, 136–7
Hatamen Gate, 16–7
Hatamen Street, 21, 25–6, 55, 94, 96, 103, 132
Hewlitt, Sir Meyrick, 132
Hillier, Edward G., 124–5
The Hongkong and Shanghai Bank, 38, 108, 123–5,
   147
Hostel of Tributary Nations, 24
Hôtel de Pékin, 37, 51, 136

Hubu Street, 19, 94

Imperial Academy (Hanlinyuan), 20–1
Imperial Army, 7, 53–4, 60, 65
Imperial Canal (Yuhe), 13, 17, 24–5, 35, 97, 104, 106, 113, 142
Imperial Court, 34, 45, 108
Imperial Decree, 63, 87–8
Imperial Edict, 52, 54, 61
Imperial Maritime Customs 21, 25, 61, 89, 122, 136, 147
Imperial Ministry of Revenue, 78
Imperial Palace, 2, 13, 16–17
Imperial Summer Palace (Yuanming Yuan), 11, 15
International Relief Forces, 63–5, 67, 70, 99, 104

Jardine, Matheson & Co., Ltd., 38, 128–9, 147
Joostens, M., 8
Jordan, Sir John Newall, 134

Kates, George, 113–15, 118
Kiakhta Treaty, 22
Kierulff, P., 129–130
Kierluff & Co., P., 37, 130
Knobel, F.M., 82
Komura, Jutaro, 82
Kow-tow (koutou), 3–6

Land Commission, 95
Legation Clause, 9–11
Legation Guards, 51, 58, 97, 101–2, 119, 122
Legation Street, *also see* Eastern Lane of the
Mingling of Peoples (Dongjiaomin Xiang), 13, 17–9, 22–5, 32–3, 36, 54, 71, 93, 99, 101, 103–4, 106–8, 112–13, 116, 123–6, 128–9, 143, 145–7, 149–51
Legation Volunteers, 52, 59
Legations
    Austria, 58, 138
    Austria–Hungary, 15, 25, 108, 119, 120, 141, 143, 148
    Belgium, *v*, 15, 25, 26, 58, 107–8, 115, 119, 143
    Brazil, 119
    Cuba, 120
    Denmark, 119
    France, 15, 24–25, 37, 50, 55, 58, 107–8, 114–15, 119, 121, 143, 148
    Germany, 15, 24, 37, 56, 74, 76, 108, 119, 124, 126, 129, 143, 149

Great Britain, 9, 15, 17, 18, 20–2, 25, 34–7, 50, 57–63, 67, 72–3, 79, 96–100, 105–6, 115, 118–19, 121, 132–3, 137–8, 143, 147, 150
Italy, 15, 25, 97, 104–5, 118–19, 132–3, 147
Japan 15, 24, 54, 78, 97–8, 105–6, 115, 119, 121, 125, 144
Mexico, 120
Netherlands, 15, 23, 58, 101–3, 115, 117, 119, 149
Norway, 120
Peru, 120
Portugal, 119
Prussia, (demand for Legation), 14
Russia, 15, 22–4, 70, 72, 99, 101, 119, 126, 128, 147
Soviet Republic, 5, 120
Spain, 15, 24, 37, 81, 104, 119, 143
Sweden, 119
United States, 15, 19, 23–4, 34, 37, 62, 70, 79, 96, 101–2, 114, 119, 143, 150
Uruguay, 120

Li Hong-zhang, 81, 87
Liang Palace, 22
Lin Zexu, 7

Macartney, Lord, 4
MacDonald, Sir Claude, 52–3, 59, 62, 65, 79, 80
Mao Zedong, 142
Matteo Ricci's Southern Cathedral (Nantang), 18
Mongol Quarter, 21–2, 99
Morrison, Dr G.E., 54, 137, 138
Morse, H.B., 77, 86, 92, 151

The New Republic, 137
No. 14 State Guest-house, *iv*
Norman, Henry, 29, 31, 32
The North China Herald, 49–50
Northern Cathedral (Beitang), 18, 66

Peele, Thomas, 138
Peking Club, 37, 144
Peking Who's Who of 1922, 119–21, 133
Peter the Great, 22
Prince Qing, 81
Prince Kung, 19
Prince Sihanouk, 148
Prince Su, 24, 104
Protocol of 1901 (Boxer Protocol), 85–91, 94–6, 100, 104, 109, 113, 116, 119, 122, 143

Prussian Treaty, 21

Qianmen, 15–7, 69, 94, 96

Raggi, Marquis Salvago, 82
Rapkin, J., 1
Regine Building, 131
Regulations for the Expansion and Alteration of the
    Legation Quarter in Peking, 95
Reid, Arnot, 38, 124
Rockhill, W.W., 82
Rue Marco Polo, *also see* Customs Street, 25, 31,
    104, 108, 116, 144, 145
Russo-Asiatic Bank, 126

St. Michael's Catholic Church, 116, 145, 150
Samuel & Co., Ltd., 129
Sataw, Sir Ernest, 82
Savage-Landor, A.H., 49
Sennet, Freres, 131–2
Seymour, Admiral Sir Edward, 53–4
The Shanghai Mercury, 46
Smith, Reverand Arthur, 49, 70
Smith, Polly Condit, 79
Society of Righteous and Harmonious Fists
(Yihequan), 41, 46
Straight, Willard D., 137
Strong, Anna Louise, 147
Sugiyama, Mr, 54
Supreme People's Court, 23

Tartar City, 15–7, 19, 23, 25, 32, 64–5, 93–4, 96–7,
    101–2, 107

Theroux, Eugene, 138
The Times, 54, 136–7
Tianjin Treaties of 1858, 14, 23
Titsingh, Mr, 4, 5
Treaty of Nanjing, 7–8
Treaty of Tianjin, 9–11, 14, 23
Trevor-Roper, Hugh, 138
Twenty–One Demands, 115

Van Braam, Mr, 4–5
Varé, Daniele, 133
Vetch, Henri, 132
von Ketteler, Baron, 54–7, 75–6, 86, 126, 127
von Ketteler, Baroness, 76
von Rahden, Baron, 79
von Schwartzenstein, A. Mumm, 81–2
von Wahlborn, M. Czikann, 82
von Waldersee, Count, 76–8

Ward, Mr, 10–11
Water Gate (Shuiguan), 17, 64–5, 104
Williams, Dr S.S., 24

Xu Tong, 108

Yokohama Specie Bank, 125–6, 150
Yuan Shikai, 137

Zongli Yamen, 21, 34, 35, 51, 55–6, 62, 75–6, 81,
    148

Map 3. The Legation Quarter in 1915

1. British Legation
2. Italian Legation
3. Ex-Austrian Legation
4. Japanese Legation
5. Customs
6. Peking Club
7. Customs
8. Customs
9. Office Building
10. French Barracks
11. German Hospital
12. German Camp
13. French School
14. Post
15. French Legation

16. German Legat
17. Belgian Legati
18. Former Germa
19. Customs
20. Jardine, Mathe
21. Japanese Barr
22. Yokohama Spe
23. Spanish Legati
24. Annex of Japa
25. Hotel des Wag
26. Hongkong & S
27. French Hospita
28. Russian Legati
29. Site of Russian
30. USA Legation

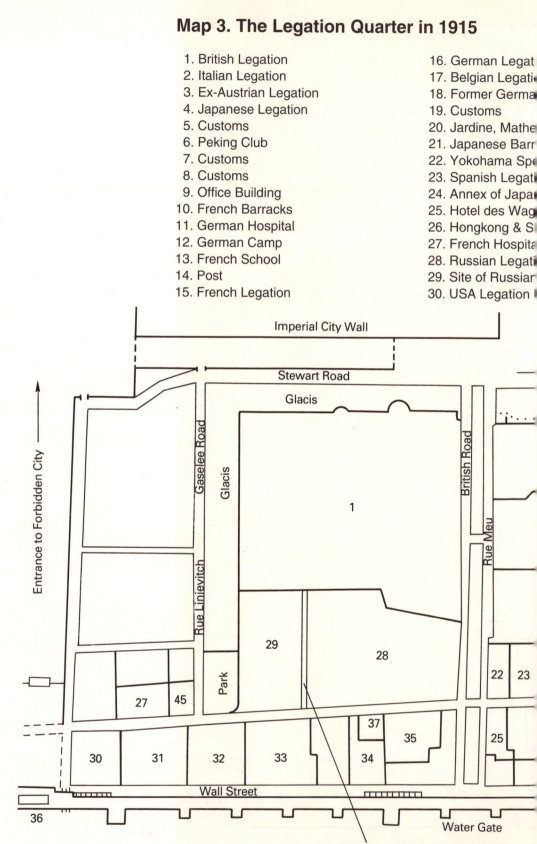

Imperial City Wall

Stewart Road

Glacis

Gaselee Road

Glacis

Entrance to Forbidden City

British Road

Rue Meu

Rue Linievitch

1

Park

29

28

22 23

27 45

37

35

25

30 31 32 33 34

36

Wall Street

Water Gate

USSR Embassy Compound Lane (after 1917)